How Did I Get Here?

HOW DID I GET HERE?

A STORY OF INTERSPECIES INTIMACIES
—(IN NEPALESE ELEPHANT STABLES)—

KIM IDOL

Westphalia Press
An Imprint of the Policy Studies Organization
Washington, DC
2019

LEAVING HOME

FACEBOOK POSTING

It's not where I'm headed that freaks me out (as much) as all the details I will be leaving behind when I go. Who will take out the trash, feed the dog, make sure the dog gets his meds., water the cats, water the plants, make sure the water softener is filled with salt, know about the kinks in the dishwasher and the dryer, pay the bills on time the way I do, keep the place clean, be on the look out for in-door scorpions so the pets don't get hurt, dust the place, keep up with the mail, keep the air conditioner working, know where the handyman's number is, know which vet to pick if the pets need to go ... know where all the stuff is and all the instructions are?

Do you know where I keep the first aid kit and the extra paper towels? Do you know which towels are for drying people and which are for cleaning up vomit?

How will life continue in my home if I leave? This sounds like a god complex to me. What will happen if I don't remain HERE fixed, tensed, perched like something frozen mid-flight at the prow of a ship, ready to react?

Bet you didn't know the power that I hold over all existence. It's been me all along that's kept the universe churning on. And I'm always, only, barely keeping up. I'm a tiny piece of the universe, but what if every tiny piece is essential? CRAP.

Off to Nepal. With a printout of an email from a man called Bhima who has arranged my trip to the elephant stables and organized my initial reservations.

With a green notebook, a yellow notebook, a camera, my laptop, Joseph Campbell's *The Power of Myth* and intermittent access to FACEBOOK.

NOTES TO HOUSESITTER

- Always close downstairs bathroom door because Seamus will get trapped inside and eat the doorframe—close the door firmly.
- Trash comes Wednesday. Recyclables every other Wednesday.
- Mortgage and student loan payment instructions are under your computer.
- Water plants on Monday, one cup of water each.
- Emergency numbers are on a list in the kitchen underneath the microwave.
- Pest control comes the 16th. You have to let them in. Summer is scorpion season.
- Empty mailbox once a week or they will stop delivering mail.
- Pay bills on the first—list is by my computer.
- Make sure you lock the garage door.
- Switch cats from upstairs to downstairs rooms (and downstairs to upstairs rooms) each day—water filters are underneath the kitchen sink, kitty litter is by each box.

- Instructions for dishwasher and washer/dryer are taped to the machines.

- Numbers and addresses for places I am staying are on the back door. Can't say for certain when I will be there though but they will be able to find me.

- List of vets you should avoid or use is on refrigerator.

- Car insurance information is in a folder by living room bookshelf.

- Call Brian for handyman emergencies. His number is on the fridge.

- Only use the left sink in the kitchen.

- Turn on front porch light after dark.

- Anti-anxiety if you have to board the dog is in pantry above the cracker shelf.

- Light bulbs are in the skinny room dresser.

- Clean sheets in plastic container upstairs linen closet.

LAS VEGAS AT MCCARRAN AIRPORT

I'm early. I'm always early because I always run screaming through airport hopped up like the bomb is on its way and I need to get airborne before an EMP pulse brings us down. A few other people are scattered about the seats by the gate locked into their electronics. No, there is no good to personal computers, cell phones, Gameboys, none of it. There is no good reason for all of us, any of us, to have portable computers. Stop. Just fucking stop! And stuff the virtual reality succubus back into the bottle.

I am reminded of the guest dingus who lectured on Gilgamesh last week. He focused on the magic of the written word. (He also had an unexplained hard on for accountants.) Excited about, "this new phase of communication" (Tweets, Twitters, Texts,

3

etc.), he just shrugged his narrow shoulders when someone mentioned how fucked up it was that constant, instantaneous, non-interpersonal communication was making us dumber and meaner. If he were a dying bud on a poisoned rose bush he'd just be thrilled to be dropping to the ground because it was a new thing.

I am soothed by the very human sound of a woman SCREAM-ING. She's missed her connection and it sounds like it's her fault, but I still like that she's just fucking out loud upset. We should all be less placid about missed connections although I'm not espousing violence, not just yet. The rest of us try to ignore the woman's high-pitched shrill of sadness, the desk clerk locks into coping mode and continue to glare at our electronics as if the secret of life lies within. I am reading this 10 novel series set in between WWI and WWII that begins with an enraged veteran blowing up a chunk of sidewalk and himself. I read half-heartedly because I find that listening to someone else scream really relaxes me. It mirrors my inner tension. Don't stop. I say, yell louder.

Seamus, the dog, gave me his best hang your head hound dog look as I walked out the door and left him behind. Sean, the husband, was snotty on the ride over, but recovered himself at the curb. The last thing my boss said to me was, "customs will be a bitch when you want to come back." She also predicted that I would return home more confused and stressed out than ever. It's only three weeks so I presume there is a limit on how depressed I am supposed to get, but thanks. I'm gonna open up *The Power of Myth* and make fun of it for a while. WOW I LOVE THIS PEN!!!!

LAX

The children are staring at me. Animated banners and wall wraps tug at my peripheral vision, one features a bouncing ball and an accompanying song. The song is not synched with the ball so it's super annoying. It's sunset. Sean should be breaking his Ramadan fast right now so he's stopped texting. Yes, I think the whole ritual is stupid as are some of mine, but mine are better and yours are stupid. Particularly galling to me is the Muslim business of not touching a woman or a dog after wudu. It's extra maddening when my husband who knows better follows this practice. This is the only flight to China tonight so the waiting area is filling up fast. Might need more coffee. Giggling kiddie iPads booting up as children their faces suffused with digital glow, fixate while Daddy seeks the toilet and Mom texts. Campbell's a bit of a sexist turd. I always feel like I am coming home when I am in L.A. An unwarranted sense of safety washes through me. I lived here a long time. Good things happened to me here, but I was always horribly unhappy. It's not a real place to me anymore. My memories of it are more real. Like last week when I talked to Elisabeth, a friend I haven't seen in years, I felt refreshed as if I'd been missing her. Clarity, clean sentences, and straight forward intentions. Less than two hours later she posted an article about bullet proof backpacks in America and wrote about how happy she was to have escaped this shitty country. Then I remembered she was a bigot and then I remembered that losing hold of that friendship was like losing weight. I need protein. I have oranges, but I need protein. Also where the hell is Guangzhou and why does my plane ticket say that it's in CAN?

Okay, (*The Power of Myth*) now Campbell is ascribing a kind of graciousness to religious blood sacrifices. I can see the difference between respecting death and lining a group of living beings onto a conveyor belt, but it's still murder and I am still disgusted.

On the plane, after we are all slotted into our padded pods, I spot the two babies who will be babbling and screaming for the next twelve hours. I predict the Chinese kid is going to be the screamer. The Hispanic one looks chiller. I can't straighten my legs. I can't curl up. I can't sleep sitting up. The goddamn seat does NOT recline ENOUGH. What horrors await me on Sky Television? I'm an integrated piece of the flying machine. I am Neo before the red pill. I'd write more but I can't see in the dark, I can't find my light switch and they turned off the lights after they fed us (the way you feed livestock). Go Southern China Airlines. Course it's all good as long as the plane stays in the air. The day before 9/11 I sat in a plane feeling unmoored and uncomfortable, just like now. Then, like now, I couldn't sleep because my mind was hamstering. I also remember feeling fat and soft. I was heading home to my husband and my dogs, but we lived with my grandmother in her house of human horrors at the time so it would be a nasty homecoming. The next day as I watched smoke pour out of the towers on the television set, my boss called to say the Dulles flight that I'd transferred off of was one of the downed planes. Three days later my husband and I went to the Inkslingers' Ball and, as usual, spent money we hadn't intended to spend. Someone pointed a camera at me and my new tattoo when we won second prize. These events were followed by American invasion of a country I was certain we would never invade because people were marching in the streets. No one thought it was a good idea and somehow I thought that would be all we needed. All this is running through my mind as I try to get comfortable.

Shit, I lost my neck pillow when I got up to stand in line for the toilet. Why are we so super polite when we are waiting for the toilet? The Chinese mother with the fat crying baby boy passes through. She's gotten zero sleep. The baby only shuts up when it's being carried. I have slept. I dreamed of Pickle Rick except the drama was set in a composition class in which I dealt 5 cards to every five students who didn't look like my students, but who I recognized. I told them to relate the cards to the play we had read whose name I could not recall but if I thought about Nicole Kidder (who had just died) my students could remember the title. I knew the lesson was stupid yet the students seemed engaged. One group showed me a butterfly they'd constructed out of wire, cucumber pieces and electric current. It was beautiful and it wiggled and although we couldn't say how it related to the play we were all thrilled. Joseph Campbell. Now that I've got all his theories in my head about dreams it all strings together. This one was about Pickle Rick. From pickle to cucumber (from which you get pickles) and forgetting the play's title because I feel dozy and clotted in my head and I am afraid of what I can't figure out and about what Sean might forget to do while I am away. As for how I felt about the class, that's easy. I forever fail my students in my estimation.

I just spoke the words I am writing out loud.

The mother with the Chinese baby looks old.

I've only watched three movies this trip. Tried to sleep. 15 hours on this plane. 2.5 to be spent at the airport on layover and then few more flying hours to reach Kathmandu. Two days there followed by a five-hour bus ride into Chitwan. This after being sick for seven days prior to leaving the U.S., after my dogs were sick for four days prior to my leaving. (There was an ugly moment in the lobby of the veterinarian's office). Watch Kim meltdown. Clients videotaped it on their phones so if you catch up with one of them... Sleeping and eating right should be my game plan for this trip. The Hispanic baby is indeed an on/off sleeper. A bunch of us wait forever outside the bathrooms again. "What the fuck are you doing in there?" KNOCK, KNOCK GODDAMMIT! The strolling mother steps out and apologizes as her baby begins to cry again. "Don't worry, we understand" I told her as we passed each other in the too small passage. My breath stinks. I have to whiz again.

Lights on. Southern China Airlines feeds you less often. That's fine but I could always use more water. Too bad I have the window seat. I have to go to bathroom every half hour.

FLYING OUT OF CHINA

Hey Baby, it's still dark outside. We just finished breakfast, which included three cups of liquid. The plane is shaking. The guy next to me has found another seat so now I have three seats to myself and I have his neck pillow, which is good because some fuck stole mine. The attendants are pushy. I think they don't know enough English so they just reach across your lap and shut the window shades or bark Chinese phrases at you before they physically direct your movements. Hey, they got things to do. I suspect their supervisor is an asshole.

40 minutes to landing and suddenly they *can* speak English

"Is there a passenger aboard with medical training? A passenger needs assistance." A young couple hurries forward behind one of the *stewardesses* (YES I SAID IT! The PC term is attendants. I KNOW!!!). I see a woman in her seat breathing from an oxygen tank as I head for the door.

Unfriendly TSA-type motherfuckers in China. Three white-gloved hobgoblins wordlessly force us through security. Can a guy be an asshole and polite at the same time? Got my pillow back (like that's a huge plot point). It's muggy and hot inside the airport, I weave my way through bunches of stressed people rushing to their connections.

Back on another plane. Watch four movies I would never have watched anywhere else. You have to be careful when you pick, too emotional and you're trapped in a very small place with no escape. Too fucking boring—well that takes you to the angry place. *Philomena*—is about a bent over backwards victim. "Thank the evil nuns for making you feel like shit." *Spotlight*—can you really yell at your editor like that and live? Are journalists really that shocked about real stuff? *Last Flags* or some such nonsense ... EH. And of course I had to watch Tony Stark blow shit up while in the real world I'm holding my breath every time I think about it. And I still don't' know what part of China I just left behind.

I guess you've had your morning meal, prayed and gone back to sleep. Be nice to the cats especially Rip. Remember Seamus is only a dog and my best boy and I'm glad not to be around for your Ramadan irritating man episodes. In fact this business of me leaving on the first day of Ramadan and you returning home after Id is excellent. I think I'm beginning to smell. My deodorant broke. I only have one orange left in my backpack.

CAN TO KATHMANDU

10 MINUTES!!!!! WHAT THE HELL ARE YOU DOING IN THERE?!! This time while waiting, legs crossed, for the person inside the bathroom stall to finish doing what the fuck ever, I stare at the Exit. Can you really, if you wanted, pull that lever and open a door midflight? Is it really that easy? I look around to see who else might be physically capable of losing their cookies and turning this flight into a group free fall. This leg of the flight is filled with more talkative female European types. The pair behind me is babbling in a way that suggests they intend to keep it up all the way to Kathmandu. Not interesting stuff, just words and words and words. The sky can't decide if it's stormy or not and the day is either hot or cold. This wordy bitch behind me has hit all the UNESCO sites. She also knows where all the ATMs are in each country because it pays to know the local culture. Blondie in the seat next to me is silent as are those passengers sitting across the aisle, but the idjits behind me are buzzing like hammering wasps. Oh good, now she is onto how cool her travel pillow is.

I remember when you lived in Jeddah and how you always looked like you were melting whenever we Skyped. I wonder what the hell I am doing and why? It's not a desperate question, just an idle one. I miss you. I miss your irritating travel presence. I haven't traveled alone overseas since we've been together. It's good to have space, but I haven't had it like this for years.

I ask for coffee and again I get sweet with cream. I can't read anymore because my eyes hurt. Feeding time again. Cows are stamping and lowing in their stalls. I like, much to my dismay, Campbell's understanding of time and transcendence. He really digs the grunting bloodied little boys into men ceremonies. But he sees the process of girls becoming women as a passive process. Women, according to Campbell are super passive beings. **She**'s more "natural" so she requires less agency. BARK. BARK. At least he doesn't turn **her** into a sinner. He says that our religions are greying snakeskins that we should have shed long ago. He explains the Heart Sutra really well. He loves the mystery of the old faiths but he thinks we need new myths that would service modern societies better. I realize that I am now back in the land of the Buddhists and thus vegetarian meals. "I'll have the fish." The woman in front of me is now explaining her husband's failure to expand his consciousness and how it's affecting their sex life. I'd rather wonder than know exactly what's going on with some people.

KATHMANDU

Muggy. Dusty. Busy and incredibly dense. People wearing face-masks, traffic cops snappily dressed and covered in soot. Congested streets. Men hurling sandbags into trucks. Boys holding hands. Girls holding hands. Dogs dozing. Jacaranda trees lining the streets, utility poles sporting thick snares of electric cable, tin can taxis, motorbikes, ancient bicycles.

My driver takes my bag and leads me across the parking lot to a battered, mud spattered vehicle.

Hey Baby! I've arrived! A guy waving a "Kim Idol" sign picked me up at the airport and then we picked up two other women and two young men on the way to Bhima's hotel. It's a house, like all the others, narrow and high. Four stories, five if you count the roof where we go to escape the heat. There are four rooms to each floor with private patios and bathrooms. The big water bottle is on the third floor essential because we can't drink the water here. I'm wide awake. It's not yet noon, but I've been traveling for a whole day and my time sense is out of whack. We retreat to our rooms after a quick meet and greet, but unlike the others I don't want a shower. I nod at Alex from So. Cal. who is availing himself of internet access which can only be achieved in the hallways and take the stairs that spiral upwards towards a spatial view of a hundred narrow buildings and small fields, patches of green where the locals grow beans, cabbage, potatoes, lentils, rice, squash, and corn. Dogs howl and bark, prayer bells ring, crickets and cicadas are chirping and buzzing and frogs are croaking, but at least here off the main streets, and amid the muddy lanes that run the length of the vegetable fields we can't see or hear the traffic. Muddy water drains down the dusty roads, feeds the plants, and coats feet, tires, the hems of our pants, the hems of saris, and sprays every vehicle that speeds through. It is scooped up, filtered and used to clean clothes, the constant task here. Women squat in the dirt and scrub and then hang their laundry outside to dry. Brilliant colored clothing even down to the underwear, no grey or black or dull whites. Clotheslines streak across the landscape along the buildings and fences. Clothing is hung in age groups. A string of children's socks decorate the patio. Beneath them men's t-shirts, then towels. Dresses swing from makeshift hangers drafting in the wind. The slow pace of life masks some fierce realities. The three women crouching together squeezing, beating and scrubbing fabrics sit underneath the shadow of a grey guard tower where a single soldier waits next to a rifle mounted on a pivot. Another tower on the opposite side of the field stands next to an ammunition dump. Smoke, from an outdoor crematorium on the hill, billows across the valley. Dogs lay strewn across the landscape in bunches. They shift from total stillness into instant action in sudden transformative jolts. There are several dog packs here, lots of growling and stalking, but no blood spilled.

I can see the Monkey Temple from the roof where Rhesus Macaque Monkeys, light brown, small to mid size beasts, abound.

"Used to be all jungle here," Bhima says. "When it was cut back, the monkeys adapted. Be careful if you visit the temple," he warns. "They are smart and strong and they steal." While I watch someone drops food on the ground and monkeys I didn't even know were there flash forward and fight for the scraps. I can see evidence of a pecking order and family groups although the hierarchy only seems to matter when something is at stake. DUH.

The next morning after being assured that the temple is within walking distance I fill my water bottle, grab my camera and set out. As I walk uphill, (How in the hell can everything be uphill?) I want to know who built the sidewalks. They just stop in places and suddenly you are standing in the street or they're four feet higher than the street. They are of different widths and shapes and some crumble to pieces when use them. Fearful of the traffic, I keep looking over my shoulder as I weave through the groups of men, women, dogs, motorbikes, buses and cars that are all meandering down the wrong motherfucking side of the road at a deceptively easy pace. 365 steps to the Monkey Temple. Vendors line the stairs on either side. If you stop you are swarmed. "Madam," four people say as they try to hand me things. "Just walking," I say waving them away. "But Madam," one women says as if I've chosen to kick her off a bridge. "When I come back," I reply. But she knows how many vendors stand between me and the top of the steps. She knows that if she doesn't get to me now someone else probably will. Up top is a disappointment. The shrines are worn and covered in waxy residue and there's a vendor stall in between each temple. The monkeys eat the alter offerings and most of the time no one seems to care until suddenly some man gets annoyed and angrily brushes interlopers away. I do buy things at the top, but I remember my lady when I return to the lower steps, which is why I will buy six sets of prayer flags when I need none. I don't really want to buy anything and although I brought my camera I don't want to take pictures either. I just want to be here.

All the travelers at this hostel eat their meals together on the roof. We bond quickly. Suddenly I am connected with a group of total strangers who share my sense of adventure. We easily share stories and personal information that we wouldn't necessarily tell our friends at home. You are suddenly part of a community and you depend on one another and then just as suddenly you hit the end of the trail and speed away from each other. "Hi" "Good luck, let me have your FACEBOOK address." "Bye!"

This group is mostly comprised of people younger than me who are on their gap year. I prefer this. It keeps me from running into couples and people who may be closer to my age and experience level, but who don't understand why I travel or why I prefer to travel rough.

Bhima's sister and wife cook the meals and serve us. The English speakers own the dinner conversation this first night. I don't know if it is because we share the same language or because of how fast and furiously we talk, but I feel the need to shut up and listen. Sandy an energetic Swiss dumpling who has just finished braiding her hair sits next to me as she is now ready to eat. Like me and the two other American women at our table, she intends to go into the Chitwan National Park to tend elephants and to volunteer at the local schools. Two twenty something Venezuelan brothers, both part way through some form of MBA sit at their own table. They remind me what it's like to be young and very sure of yourself.

"We will go to Lukla soon and trek to Everest Base camp next," the older one says finishing off their introductions.

"I'm excited about being totally immersed with English speakers," Sandy says.

"I am on a spiritual journey," Leslie, an older, British woman, says. "I miss my family, but my husband and my daughters totally understand."

"What do you do?" Sandy asks her.

Leslie hesitates "I am a Reiki practitioner, a shamanist. I don't like to put myself in a category, really."

"And what are you doing here?" Leslie asks Alex the man who was playing with the Internet on the third floor and who is now scooping mouthfuls of dal off his plate. "I'm from So. Cal.," he says in between bites. "Traveling for fun. Tutoring English now and in a couple of days I'm going to a 10 day retreat."

Bhima and his family run the hotel and inhabit the first floor apartments. I suspect the whole extended family has heavily invested economically and personally in this endeavor and know how lucky they are to have achieved so much.

"What's up with the guns," I ask pointing towards the soldier shacks. "There is sometimes trouble, "Bhima says. He is a soft-spoken guy.

"What kind?" Sandy asks.

"We sometimes have trouble with the militia and the communists," he replies. "The soldiers pulled me off a bus the last time when they knew I was a Communist and held me over a cliff while they asked questions. Then they dropped me over it." His English is mucky, but I think he just said that they threw him off the cliff when they were done and still he sits at the head of this table fantastically physically whole and prosaically serving us rice pudding and potatoes like that's still important. None of the American women eat enough to satisfy him, but we come from the land of *Reviving Ophelia*. We've been competing with skinny girls all our lives. Now that the topic has been broached, the Nepalese men discuss revolution among themselves as if it's a normal something slipped into the daily calendar now and again.

How are you, Baby? I keep wondering about you at home with the dogs muttering your way through Ramadan. This place seems exactly the same as when you and I were last here. On the surface this all feels familiar and I wonder if travel just does that. It makes everywhere feel like home.

"When where you here last?" Leslie asks me.

"Eight years ago," I reply. "When we trekked to the Everest Base Camp." We don't spend too much more time up top talking as suddenly everyone is beginning to fad as jet lag settles in.

The next morning, I am up before anyone else and I come up top to write and look around. Bhima's wife is there. She brings me a cup of Nescafé indicating where I will find the sugar before she goes back downstairs. If I look across the valley think I see the top of a temple. Foliage obscures most of the structure, the jungle isn't all gone, and even at 5 a.m. a long line of people are streaming up the road towards it before they vanish into the trees that conceal the bulk of the structure. Higher up on the mountain I see patches of brick through the trees suggesting the presence of a monastery.

"They are circling the stupa seeking grace," Bhima says joining me at the wall. "The more times you circle, the more grace you have." The people keep flowing towards the temple and disappear into the trees until mid-morning when the heat and the humidity begin to rise precipitously.

The two American women leave without saying good-bye.

Bhima suggests a city tour for the rest of us. In addition, the Venezuelans, Leslie, Sandy and I agree to venture into the Tamal shopping mall today. It's rows and rows of shops catering specifically to tourists and anything bought there is more expensive than you can get anywhere else, but we need supplies, rain jackets, under armor, etc. I need a second shirt. I only brought what I wore on the plane plus a raincoat and a bulky down jacket that I already regret. Why, oh why, didn't I bring my microfleece instead? On the way to Durbar Square (a plaza filled with temples, idols, fountains, goats and palaces) we all describe the places we've been. Everyone in the group has traveled far and wide.

And then later while we walk, Leslie and I climb to the top of a set of stairs and sit. She doesn't buy much in the way of souvenirs but I can tell that every piece of jewelry she wears was bought here or in India. She also has succumbed to the temptation to get henna tattoos. Hindu patterns run up both her arms. I too have begun morphing. The shirt I now wear was bought off a vendor and looks like nothing I could find at home. We are eating popsicles and they are melting onto our hands faster than we can eat them. Neither of us care.

"You don't have a camera," Leslie says handing me a piece of tissue.

"I still don't really want to take pictures," I say. "Picture taking removes me from the experience. Last time we were here I took about a thousand photographs but I just don't feel like it this time."

"I'm writing it all down," Leslie says.

"Me too, but I seem unable to get down to the deeper details. It's all surface bullshit."

"Yes! Mine reads like a school girl's diary just now."

"I guess we keep writing anyway."

"I guess so." Half of her popsicle separates from the rest and drops to the ground. Without hesitation she picks it up and pops it into her mouth.

I look out at the plaza and realize that I miss Sean deeply while revisiting places we visited together years ago.

As a group we spend the rest of the day at different historic sites, some of them are laid low by the recent earthquakes. Some temples have been fortified with scaffolding while men work to reconstruct a couple thousand years of history, but the damage done is not as extensive as I'd imagined.

"It was more in the mountains," Bhima says. "The people there lost much."

The rains come as we eat lunch on an outdoor patio. We collect our plates and run for cover. Leslie, Sandy and I discover that we are all animal obsessives. We share stories about animals, animals we've saved, lost and regretfully, didn't help at all. On the ride to Tamal the whole group shares broken bone stories. One fractured patella (snowboarding "off road"), one two-story stairway tumble, a broken hand, a broken foot, a broken tibia, and one broken arm. As a 4-year old Sandy attempted a springing handstand from a chair. The older brother who broke his knee says that he had to crawl back to the main slope so that insurance would cover the cost of his surgery. The young men are bright boys, moral boys at least they seem so. The kind you hope money creates. Leslie, who would probably annoy the hell out of me if I'd met her anywhere else, tells us more about her shamanistic journey. She believes in destiny. I don't. We're both okay with that. She's just emerged from India. Sandy says she just likes to travel. At home she teaches little children to ride and care for horses. She reminds me of a Swedish girl I met on safari in Botswana. Like that girl, Sandy seems meek, but she is not. She and I worry that when we finally get to see the elephants we will see that they are being mistreated. Our jeep rolls over a piece of road that crumbles under the weight of the car and the driver expertly navigates it while the rest of us grab something to keep our balance.

The rains don't stop by the time we finish lunch so we give a trip to the river a pass (I don't know why, really. It was Bhima's edict) and we fell back on Tamal. By the end of the day after sharing travel plans we know that the brothers who are spending a few more days in Kathmandu have decided to join Alex and teach English before they head to Lukla and that Leslie has decided to attempt the trek to the base camp, on her own, personally guided trip. It was a good day even with the rain. Time has begun to become unimportant. I don't know how many hours we've spent wandering the city. I don't know how close we are to dinner. I don't know what day it is. Bhima drops us off at the mall and someone else will keep track of the time because I can't be trusted for one thing.

"The rains are coming early," Bhima observed as we climb back into the car just ahead of another downpour. The rain comes and goes and brings the dust down so the air is cleaner and cooler. On the drive back to the hostel the young men, at Leslie's urging, explain that they are from Venezuela, but live in Columbia. They go on to describe what the fuck happened to Venezuela, a country that was until very recently on the way up and that is in shambles now, in a way that I finally understand.

"Our family runs many businesses," the older one says, "but mainly we are ranchers in the dairy business. Years ago our grandfather turned vegan and changed the way we ranch."

"Humanely," the younger one adds.

"And now all our family does the same," the older one says.

So all five of us are vegans or vegetarians. All five have traveled and all five are curious and fairly confident people with stories to tell—nice.

I retreat to my room when we return. The view from my porch is also fantastic. By late afternoon, the valley echoes with the sounds of children ordering one another about during play. Occasionally motorbikes putt through and Hindu music drifts upwards from a radio downstairs. I can also hear feet in flip-flops passing back and forth in the lanes. The soldiers manning both towers are relaxed and chatting while they eat. The women now done with their fieldwork are resting against the brick walls that mark the edges of their properties while one lean old man laboriously finishes churning a barren muddy patch, by hand, with a short handled shovel. Of course the birds are busy. A dozen bright blue jobs are taking advantage of the fact that the man turns up seeds as he digs. He stands amid a speckled patch of brown soil and blue birds as he works his way through his yard.

The only animals I don't pity here are the birds. The rest break my heart.

Sandy and I have a 5 a.m. start tomorrow for a five hour bus ride. We say our good-byes at dinner to people we will never see again except on FACEBOOK.

"You must be ready on time," Bhima says.

"It's a five hour drive?" I ask.

"It's more like," he shrugs, "a seven hour drive." That is Nepalese for, could be a freaking 9 to 15 hour drive, who's to say? "Stretches of road are under construction," he continues, "the driver means to avoid the traffic by leaving early."

I spend the night on the porch working my way through Campbell's *Power of Myth* to the enveloping sound of crows cawing. They've settled on all the rooftops and in the trees. I love the sound. It's harsh and honest. Can't explain it any better. Somewhere around eleven, I start reading Harlan Ellison. Sadly then,

I give in to a headache. I haven't read so much in a long time. So I turn on the television, locate the one English station and watch *Rogue One*. It's a better film when you don't pay for it although a CGI Carry Fisher is super creepy. Drifting to sleep I wake up at 2, read more, write more and then I type out "Shattered Like a Glass Goblin" for no known reason, all the while remembering Ellison's scathing critique, "Pay the writer." Then because I heard him deliver that particular speech in a documentary in which Robin Williams interviewed him I am sharply reminded of sitting in a white high rise hotel room in India when I learned that Williams had killed himself. Sean locked down and waxed pragmatically about the death and I spent the next few hours on the Internet hunting every available shred of information I could find trying to make sense of the thing. I didn't know Williams of course, but we adopted the same protocols when Sydney died. I lay on the floor sobbing while Sean graded papers. With the recent death of his uncle, Sean's retreated inside again. He says he hasn't had time to consider grieving. I'm certain that will blow back on me the moment he finally unloads. He'll accuse me of not caring and of being self centered and the fact that I asked several times whether he was okay won't be remembered. He's got this weird amnesia. Sometimes I think I should keep a record of our conversations. I've even started a couple of times. Then I get bored with the idea and delete them. What am I going to use them for, a huge SEE moment?

I don't go back to sleep but in deference to the others living here I stay in my room until sunrise.

SUNDAY: INTO THE PARK

I find Bhima first thing in order to settle my account. He lent me money on our city tour. I don't have enough cash on hand to pay him today. So, hoping he's a good guy, I give him all the credit card information he needs in order to ruin my credit history.

When I tell Sandy later on, she suggests that my ability to mess up his reputation should guarantee that he behaves.

"You should email me when you return," Bhima admonishes me. "Usually people return here after the elephant stables so they can tell me if everything was alright, but you will have to email me." He is very intense about this and during this trip he won't be the only guide/owner to insist that they be told what needs to be fixed.

I eat breakfast in Bhima's kitchen in his private apartments. Because I am up uber early I didn't expect to get breakfast, but he fries a couple of eggs and ladles them over toast. While I wait, I inspect his a bookcase that is stuffed to the gills. "I have a wide range of interests," he says, setting my plate down on the table. His extensive Nepalese and English book collection contains fiction, nonfiction, theology, Frankenstein, Raymond Chandler, a whole range of English classics, an autobiography of Dali Lama (although Bhima is not Buddhist) and several science and history texts.

Sandy gets fed too when she comes down struggling with two suitcases the size of eight year olds. Clunk, clunk, clunk as she maneuvers them down the steps.

"Have you ever had a client that was a pain in the ass?" I ask while we eat.

"Oh yes," Bhima says. "An American woman who complained about the weather when we picked her up at the airport. Then she kept the other residents awake by stomping around in her room and slamming doors all night and then she stood in that field," he points at a shuttered window, "and danced until I made her stop." I think dancing is his polite word for throwing a screaming tantrum. "I called the U.S. embassy and they told me to call the police," he says. "But I didn't want to do that. We finally returned her to the airport and I thought about closing down the hotel for good." This seems like an extreme response from a guy who was dangled over a cliff, but I suspect that Bhima detests emotional excess.

After breakfast, with Bhima's help, we grab our bags and run down a muddy road in the dark to the bus stop. "It might be a nine hour drive," Bhima says to us. "Also, it's going to be hotter where you're going. Be careful around the elephants. Pay attention to the owners."

Okaaaay. Sandy and I board while Bhima pays the driver and ensures that we know he did. As is my habit, I automatically stress about the cost although 1,000 rupees (9 dollars U.S.).

It's an onerous bus ride and very abruptly requires an unscheduled transfer. Our bus stops and the, I guess, conductor waves Sandy and me off the bus and points to a dilapidated ten-seater parked just ahead. After some discussion between conductors, the conductor of the new vehicle who doesn't seem to think we should come with him, escorts Sandy and me to two seats in the back. I sit on mine and the back breaks away.

"It's broken," I say to whoever this guy is.

"Yeah," he nods and returns to his seat up front. We are definitely HOT now. I turn on the fan, to make the hot air move and learn that Sandy doesn't like air being blown on her.

The bus navigates along a winding undone mountain road that drops away on my side of the bus, to a wide muddy river running below; it's not mud, but glacial melt clouding the water. Plastic bottles bobbing on the surface drift downstream and pile up in spots where the river slows down or collect at rocks and tree limbs big enough to resist the force of the flowing water. My mind focuses on nothing in particular. Goats tied off with string graze in out of the way places. Did we run down those dogs that seemed to run under the back wheels of the bus? How much should a slice of cucumber cost? My last orange is a messy meal. My hands are sticky. Should elephants be raised alone? They seem like family types to me. The miles roll on and I am uncomfortable, but since I don't know where we are heading nor when we should get there I just drift and watch the sky, the trees, rocks, roads, mountaintops, people, rivers, and vendor huts as they roll on by.

Our clothes are sticking to us by the time we arrive at Hotel Park Inn, our hostel in Sauhara, Chitwan. Arjun, the owner greets us and shows us our room, the last in the row. Sandy will not let anyone help her with her bags. We don't unpack. We drop our gear and head out. On our first walk into the village, Sandy takes a picture of a dead snake lying belly up on the side of the road. She says it's her first snake although to my mind a dead snake is really an un-snake. Traffic keeps to the left. Walk on the left side of the road. If you hear horns honking move more to the left and/or look behind you. The river is a half a football field to our right, wild grass, small, farmed plots and the first elephant stable I've ever seen with no elephant in sight.

Squat toilets are the custom here, but European toilets have been installed. People here use hoses to wash up after pooping or peeing. Flimsy toilet paper rolls are provided out of politeness and they don't last long. When I order coffee I am offered a small cup instead of access to a pot and it will be instant and it will be sweetened.

By the next morning the first of the dozens and dozens of bug bites I am going to get are sprouting on my legs and the stickiness that will be my lot until I leave makes the fact that I just showered a shallow memory. Billowing clothing is the best defense. Still we enjoy the cool muggy morning. The hotel mascot, a fox faced terrier named Jenny, is enjoying herself too by bopping about in the yard in a highly investigative mood. I can see the white-capped head of a farmer as he tracks through a field of what looks like corn. Kids, dogs, the sounds of staff setting up for the day add to the morning mix. Those who smoke are sitting on the porch upstairs. There are signs that forbid public smoking in the village as well as littering. Plastic trash is evil.

When the village floods as it does every season the garbage is washed into the jungle for one thing.

One of the other residents, an alien life form by my estimation, walks by dressed up to the hilt: silk scarf tied around her neck, hair braided and coiled, lots of bling, stylish shoes, well tailored pants and a groovy short jacket.

I've never seen this part of Nepal. The country has three zones, the high Himalayas, the foothills and here the lowest part, the North Indian Plain with tropical savannas like those in Chitwan. Very green and lots of water and misty mornings, nothing like any other savannah I've ever seen. The guides repeat what seems true that the monsoon season is coming early this year. By the end of this trip I will have visited all three Nepals and, except for Africa (Botswana, Zambia, Zimbabwe, Madagascar, and South Africa), it's the only place I've seen twice. I get to check my memories for accuracy, who does this for God's sake? My brain is still fogged with out of place anxieties that I simply won't release. Even in this place I hear the whining, high speed whirl of thoughts racing one after the other too fast to be properly considered or identified while I try to protect myself from feeling too lost or too sad or too angry. Maybe that changes here if I stay long enough.

SAUHARA, CHITWAN

FACEBOOK POSTING

Posting outside amid mosquito territory in the dark on off and on Internet. Finally at park. 9 hour bus ride supposed to be 7 because of car accident ... I THINK? Last part on motorcycles ... NAW we don't need helmets but hey, since I'm wearing a backpack, my camera and am trying to hold onto a water bottle too ... who cares!!!! GODDAMN it's HOT. Jungle treks and elephant stables for a bit. THEY HAVE TIGERS HERE!!!! One-horned rhinos! I feel sticky ... what is that thing in the shower? Will it be my friend if I keep it from getting wet?

AT THE INN

We eat breakfast at tables set just outside our rooms. There always seems to be someone working in the field next us cutting, bundling, clearing stalks, or turning over earth. Goats feed from what looks like a grass ball suspended from a rope. Ducks are set free in the morning and are caged at night. Chickens do whatever they damn well want. All the buildings are set off the ground three or four feet in case the place floods. We sit underneath gazeboes in the ... garden (doesn't seem like the right word). It is organized growth, but it doesn't seem cut off from the rest of the environment the way yards are at home. Gardens, fields, and forests here merge into a single organism. Now someone turns on his tractor and so the morning is officially ended and the workday has started.

The maids sweep the porches with short handled brooms that look like blond horsetails. They are small, hand held affairs that force them to stoop. I need to move because I am in the way and I need to anticipate the necessity because they won't ask.

So working in the elephant stables is a completely self-motivated enterprise. The elephant handlers follow a fluid schedule. You have to track them down and introduce yourself. According to two German women who have been here for three weeks, all four of us are assigned to tend one elephant. Young, tan, long-haired beauties, they don't speak to us until Sandy makes a point of introducing herself. According to Sandy they hate it here. They have one more week to go. They've been biding their time by hiding out in their rooms watching movies and walking to town for lunch. They don't like the elephant gig. "The elephants are very badly treated," one says and the other nods in agreement. They don't like their handler who they say "hates women," and is disrespectful. In sum, the elephants carry tourists into the jungle twice a day, have to be fed three times a day and need to be washed twice a day to cool down. They girls say that we need to be at the stables by 6 a.m. although Sandy and I were told by Arjun to come at 8. The next morning the four of us, and Arjun are driven to depot at the edge of the jungle where elephants pick up and drop off tourists. We sit there for an hour or more watching elephants and tourists come and go and watching a monkey troop play at the edges of the trees or see the trees being disturbed as the monkeys move away through the jungle 40 feet off the ground. Tips for drivers are in cash, elephants prefer fruit. One elephant can take a wad of cash and fling it overhead so that it drifts precisely into her driver's lap. As I understood it once all the morning tours return we will go to the stable. This doesn't happen. We only return to the inn once all is said and done.

Jungle trek tomorrow. I will talk to someone the day after that if things don't become more clear. I can't just hang around for two weeks. I'll lose my mind.

FACEBOOK POSTING

As always the birds are up first as is an invisible creature that clicks and seems to live just outside our front step. It's raining. Someone is already working the field. Someone else has hacked my phone number. Prophet Manassah has sent me a message, which I have bounced back and blocked. The crickets are also up sending out a shrill wall of sound and birds are cooing. It is one of the only cool moments of the day and yes there it is the sound of a rooster that always reminds me of Botswana in the suburbs where cats, donkeys, and chickens make the morning noises and I can hear some of the guests mumbling behind closed doors.

Back to the business of relying on people who don't speak English when I don't speak their language but I think you learn to listen when the flow of words is never going to come as you expect and when you know that you will not be understood as you expect.

I've been writing every day for hours and am still working my way through Campbell who to my dismay amazes me as much as he is wrong and am reading.

There's a little dog here. Of course, it's Kim writing this story so there will always be a dog involved. Jenny a white fuzzy fox faced dog defends the property. She barks and barks but she is easily disarmed. If you are kind she comes near to be scratched. The owners treat her like a pet, but initially she cringes if you move too fast, as if she is used to being swatted. The park is very near the inn and only the river sets the jungle apart from the rest of the village. I wonder how many dogs get eaten by the crocodiles. I also bet that the dogs here are croc savvy. Arjun and another guide escorted us to the river last night where we saw our first rhino stretched out half in and half out of the water. Some Aussie chick wearing faux diamond earrings, who was tramping through the woods in a white dress and black shiny sandals proclaimed that it was dead about ten times. I felt the urge to knock her into the river, but didn't. Instead I picked up a plastic bottle some ASSHOLE had dropped in the park and walked on. After we had returned to the safe side of the river, Sandy, the guides and I sat by the river and watched the sun set over the park.

Now I hear the hostel cat yowling and I wonder how cats survive here. Saw some of the elephants last night. Will start this morning to see what this elephant tending business is all about. Jeep and canoe safaris are in the offing. I have trouble not thinking of Botswanan savannahs when I wake up here.

"I miss miss miss you and am probably getting some sort of skin thing in my future because of contact with this dog but I will disinfect before I come home."

"I LOVE YOU!!!!!

I am in the way of the hotel staff who gently keep moving me aside so they can get to their jobs. I NEED COFFEE."

Went to buy a carved rhinoceros this morning and as he was wrapping it up the salesmen asked where I came from. "Trump country," he then said to me. I shook my head. And then almost as a consolation gift he said, "But Obama was good!"

It goes like this. You're wet when it's hot because it's hot and humid or it has recently rained. And it's searing hot and your clothes are wet because you're sweating or you're wet when it's raining because well .... And you're wet when you take a shower from which you will emerge feeling hot and sweaty.

Get used to it.

So I still can't get information that makes sense out of Arjun in terms of elephant interaction. And if you want some kind of schedule you can forget that. Apparently Sandy and I stole the German girls' bedroom. They left for a few days to take a side trip and when they returned we were in their room and their stuff had been moved down the row.

Sandy and I walked the length and breadth of town (she has an app. that counts her steps. I don't want to know) this morning seeking an elephant bathing experience. We want to video the event.

Walk on the left side of the road, skitter to the far left as vehicles barreling down on you from behind honk. Say, "Namaste" to everyone you pass. (Yes, yes, I bow to the light within, got to keep moving.)

Sandy and I make our first visit to the elephant stable this afternoon, but not the one where the Germans have been working. Arjun escorts us down the road to a stable that has two elephants and introduces us to three handlers who speak some English. We all know enough shared language to get by. The youngest man is tasked with paying attention to Sandy and me.

They give us pads to sit on at the stable and apportion hay and rice to each of us. We work for an hour coiling rice and hay into bricks, which we then feed to the elephants who can take up to an hour to finish eating. (100 bricks a day we are told). Despite the pads, we also sit in the straw, home to little bugs that savage my thighs and my hips, while we learn how to assemble elephant food. The children, who live in and around the stable, gather around us as we work, and talk to us as if they've known us their entire lives.

Two skinny men instruct us, while another older man and 3 small children watch. We bend, wrap, fold and tie the food bundles and place them by the elephants or hand them to a grasping trunk and then the elephants play with their food until they are ordered to eat. Given that they need to consume so much food to live, so much that the handlers sleep in the barns with the animals to be there for their middle of the night feeding I wonder if some essential instinct has been curbed by captivity. Handlers bark at the animals to make them behave and they chain them. The youngest one wears chains around both her back legs. The handlers say this is because she tends to kick out and cause harm unless they restrain both her hind feet. The men are friendly and answer all our questions. I wonder if they expect a tip, because I don't have any extra money. One handler says that he works seven days a week. I assume that means that he can only rest while the elephants are carrying tours through the park. Twice daily. I don't know what happens to the handlers' schedules during the monsoon season when the tours don't run. They don't look like unhappy people. Sandy and I work until 6:30. We are instructed to return early tomorrow morning for more food making and elephant bathing. So we return to the inn and I take another shower while Sandy goes outside to sit and write. By the time I join her and the two German girls I am informed that she has already told them anything I might need to report about our adventures at the elephant stable. I can't tell if these girls are young, arrogant or just haven't seen enough yet to be more amenable than they are.

By the time I wake the next morning Sandy has already gone to hang out with "her elephants." They were incredibly kind to us yesterday in the elephant stable. A task I am certain would have taken the men six minutes to complete, took us ages. When I look at the photographs I see that I look like a four year old try-ing to learn to tie my shoes. I left earlier than Sandy who prom-ised that she that would return to the inn in time to join me on the jungle trek. It was good to see how the animals and handlers live and good to get a semblance of hand hands on experience with the animals, but there's no joy in a job no one needs us to do. The endeavor is in reality just a tourist gig. I want more than that and the need to organize the job on a daily basis while working around the handlers' schedule, which changes from day to day, is an extra task. I'll go back, but today I want to see the jungle and I wanted to write before we go on today's trek.

Getting used to the fact that we are sharing our room with a number of small crawling animals. Moving things are on the walls, the ceiling, the floor, and in my bed. The frogs like the bathroom. The lizards like to crawl overhead, but will drop off from time to time and there's this big black bug that's close to being an ugly bird because it's so big. I've seen some snakes outside. Be prepared to hear me scream from this continent if I find one of those in my bed.

I can hear voices outside but can't tell if the women outside our window are the ones we had dinner with. Will it be weird if I open the door and stare at them?

The electricity is off which means the fan is stopped so I take a shower before I get dressed. I've been sleeping naked and happily Sandy doesn't care. "Anyway," she says, "My vision is so poor without my glasses how does it matter?"

I don't sleep much. I sweat. I read. I write. I worry about fending off the depression demon that lives in my head and waits for down time, but so far I've got it contained.

The internet does not work in the room and doesn't work at all once the electricity shuts down for the day, so I write and write. As for Sandy she walks and talks in her sleep, but nothing wakes her up. Last night, she jumped up out of bed because she felt something moving around under the sheets with her.

I dreamed about something that upset me. I don't remember what because I took too long to write it down, but it was a busy, busy dream and I was grateful to wake up because consciousness spared me from the tasks my subconscious was assigning me. Frog in the bathroom. Lizards in bath and bedroom. Birds, bugs, and lizards living in the top of the gazebo. The birds hanging upside down from the rafters peek out at us while we eat. The lizards crawl about the bamboo framework. The bugs drop onto the table and then buzz off.

Arjun instructs us to wear dull colors into the jungle. I think my camera will stay here, too much rain. Meals are all the same, dal and rice for lunch and dinner, one egg and rice or a pancake for breakfast, which is all you really want to eat.

THE JUNGLE, THE STABLE, THE VILLAGE

FACEBOOK POSTING

Pro-tip: Hiking socks are a no-go in the jungle. Leeches that live in the brush and drop off the overhead greenery, hop onto your feet and ankles, hook onto the thick weave and wind their way through to your skin.

As we leave the river and hike into the dense vegetation that closes in around us (one guide in front and another behind Sandy and I) I remember a sixth grade class trip to Idyllwild. I think because it was one of the first times I trooped through a wild place with strangers.

The guides don't mention leeches when they promote the jungle trek, but it seems that they are particularly active during the monsoon season, like now when the ground and the plants are soaking wet. I pass one just as we cross into the forest. It is clinging to a leaf stem holding its body perpendicular to the ground waving it like a flag in the wind with a blood seeking tip.

"Watch it, Madam," a guide says as if he were pointing out a problem that I might avoid with stealth.

The first time I say that I am being attacked by leeches the guides tell me to remove my shoes and socks. Then they pluck the little creatures off my bare feet and ankles laughing because these are only baby leeches. When an adult the size of a halved pencil drops on my hand and before it digs in, the guide removes it. The men don't kill any of the animals, which in retrospect is kind of cool. I force myself to accept the fact of the leeches. I want to keep trekking.

Then we see a crocodile waiting in the water with a stillness that suggests it has been there since man began to walk upright. "But it is not the dangerous kind, Madam." The ground by the river is awash with red bugs hooked together in flagrante as they race about our feet. The jungle is part wet grassland and part the Mowgli type bushy mess you see in the movies.

We hear the rhino before we see her. I can hear the thick sugarcane grass that grows higher than we are tall being parted as something heavy passes through. The blade tips waver as she moves toward the river, which she needs to cross in order to access her favorite watering hole. Then she hears and smells us. Big and graceful she lifts her head in our direction and will not approach her bathing spot while we remain. She is one of two that we see while standing in the overgrown grass. They are a whole different kind of animal in comparison to the two African types (only one now that the last wild white rhino has died). They have all the time in the world to eat and keep cool here. Poaching is nonexistent in the park. A huge military presence affects this ceasefire. Soldiers even sleep in the park. For self-defense our guides who are not allowed to carry guns, carry big bamboo poles. I am given a quick lesson on what to do depending on which predator comes after us (run or not, climb or not, make noises or not). Don't climb a tree if the elephant comes after you, but yes, if it's a rhino. If a tiger sees you, don't run confront it. Do run if it's a bear or a rhino, but not in a straight line.

600 or more types of birds. A chicken that screams like a monkey and three kinds of deer. Three spotted deer bounding through the high grass their backs and heads only visible for seconds before they disappear. Bear poop is in the high hides

we use for resting places, which means a bear spent the night there and we see a wild board nuzzling the ground for roots. The guides tell me how animals die in the park and they tell me about the people they've seen die in the park. The quieter one shows me where he's been bitten by a bear. "Life in the jungle is hard madam," he says as he leads us towards the river.

When I return to the room, I immediately wash my clothes, and rinse off the blood running down my ankles and feet. The leeches inject a coagulant into the wounds that's very effective. I also wash my hair using shampoo I stole from Sean. Why use up mine when he has some?

Sometimes I don't know why that man still loves me. ☺

Monsoon season means that every day you confront multiple weather realities. It's misty and comfortably chilly in the morning. By mid-morning we are either too warm or are being subjected to a full-bodied downpour or we are being baked dry by a blazing heat that usually prefaces the next storm. No weather front endures for long. Wear clothing that doesn't stink easily, and that dries fast.

We seek shelter in the shared shelters everyone runs to when it rains or when it's too hot to work or walk around. The tourists like the rain. They are the only ones. Although all the park animals seem to enjoy a good soak in the river, the locals and all the animals (except for the fucking leeches) hate it.

Several species here have no predators except for men and maybe their own kind, but none of them seem to lack that hyper-vigilance that keeps you alive when something wants to eat you. For the tiger, the elephant and the rhinoceros the fights are more often about territory, when they're not about sex. The tigers are solitary creatures. Their first rejection is from their mothers. The rhinos are both solitary and social creatures as are the elephants. I don't know about the bears except they seem as shy as leopards.

Apparently after the monsoon season the park rangers level the grasslands with machetes and controlled fires. This makes it easier to spot wildlife, but also I suspect this serves a natural function in terms of preserving the environment. Uncontained, the grass takes over. It was once the elephants' job to keep the jungle trimmed down, but now, not enough elephants. But now there is too much grass, and too much of a vine the Brits brought here scrambling over the landscape killing other necessary and indigenous plant life and when the rains come, the water washes the trash piled up in the human settlements into the jungle.

"There used to be hotels in the park, run by an American corporation," the guide says, "but they are gone now. They would stake goats to draw out the tigers for the guests."

"That's fully fucked up," I mutter but I am heard.

"Yes," the guide says. "It is a bad practice. It's not allowed now."

I am human, but human beings seem to be an infection that Earth needs to purge and will, but only after we've destroyed everything that isn't us so that we and every other living creature on this planet can die badly—probably from disease. And once my mind runs onto this track I begin to think of other things that stress me out. I try to block those thoughts, but every contact with the racing pulse of life at home in Las Vegas unsettles me (i.e. news and emails). There is always so much to do at home. I am always running everywhere at a fevered pace. I'd spin out if I didn't find things to do that didn't make me FOCUS. It's not a right way to live and I think it ages us. But slowing down makes me see the craziness that lives inside me. It's not just me. Civilized people are crazy people running alongside an abyss on a road that eventually tips them into it. Today, I walked. I did my laundry. I wrote. I read—that's all I needed to do. This is how the villagers here live. There's a lot of work to do and it all gets done and is never completely done, but no one rushes through everything to get to an end. But (I ask) given the choice, they want life to be "better," but they like their lives and they miss the space and the energy that goes away when too much wilderness is cut back because modernization demands it.

People here stop in the middle of one task to take a child to the bike shop and return to that task later. If a relative is sick they vanish from work until the relative is well. Most tasks are communal so someone else will step in. If someone needs a rest during the day, she/he takes it. They're doing just fine.

It's scary slowing down. I feel as if a big black dragon raises its head inside me when I do. It's a beast that breathes cyanide gas. And then suddenly I am standing on a cliff watching the thing raise its head until it is eye level with my small form. The monster is all of my own making and yet, I can't control nor kill it. It can only be bargained with. Its desire to kill me is mine. I am not suicidal, but something in me knows that I am nothing. I am the abyss. My breath comes from a hollowed out place. And then I know that time is something I imagine and the world is only what I want to believe is true. The demon dies when I do, when the energy I use to give it shape and meaning for me is used up. I never want that to happen, so I keep running ahead of that day. I keep healthy in order to put that day off. I create goals to pretend progress and to distract me from my fears. Goddamn.

Bug bites cover my legs. Last night was really miserable. As with the leeches I seem to be the only one who is being attacked insects although I haven't gone anywhere everyone else isn't going too. I slathered bug juice all over my body so now I am sticky and itchy and grimy.

I stayed in the hotel to write while Sandy returned to the elephant stables alone to see if she could help. She returned hours later, saying, "It was weird." Apparently the men there were not as welcoming as the others were yesterday. Sandy didn't recognize these new men, but kept pressing them to be able to help. Finally the young man who was there yesterday arrived and got her started building rice/straw bricks. This time, however, he became more intimate than he had the day before when Sandy and I were both present He touched her and sat very near and asked her if she was married. Sandy replied that she had a boyfriend and had been in this relationship for five years. Still the handler persisted in what seemed like flirting which Sandy thought was strange because she and we understood that the kind of touching he was doing was unseemly in Nepalese terms of polite society.

"After we were done," she paused "And there is enough elephant food for days now. He kept talking to me, asking personal questions and then he invited me to a dance that will be held tonight in the village. I asked if I could bring my friends and he replied, yes and kissed me on both cheeks before I left. I didn't want to be rude," she said, "but next time I will have to be clear because one day is okay, but I can't do that for three weeks."

My legs and feet are on fire with all the itching from the bug bites and leech punctures.

There is no way you can outmatch the colors of a half wild place. This afternoon while waiting for Arjun to come and drive me to a scanner so I that can send a picture of myself for the visa I will need for the Himalayan part of my trip, I see a line of brown women dressed in bright red saris, some of them carrying baskets on their heads, accompanying a herd of black buffalo across a bright green field of tall grass. A man dressed in white trails behind as they trek home at an easy unhurried pace as if the sun will wait until they get home before it finally falls below the horizon.

Walked into the village with Sandy last night looking for the "dance" because the young handler, who wants Sandy, invited her. She has told him that she has a boyfriend, "for five years," but that hasn't slowed him down. Sean says that she has to tell him that she is married because in this culture anyone can have one or more girlfriends, that doesn't mean you belong to anyone. I deliver this advice.

"I don't want to lie," Sandy says.

"You need to use the code words they understand," I reply.

After wandering around in the dark for hours and enjoying the walk and the night, Sandy and I come to the conclusion that either the young man lied or that she misunderstood him. Either way she's still got a problem on her hands. She's not worried about handling it, but she really shouldn't have to.

The next night it's just me and the German girls waiting for dinner. Sandy's still out with the elephants. More dal and rice, we're not anxiously waiting dinner. A group of locals, we don't know who they are, take control of the table next to us that's underneath the only gazebo with a working fan. We glower at them while we eat rice portions in the unmediated heat and wave the mosquitoes away. Moving with firm intent they load the table with a radio, a little beer, and several bottles of whiskey that they spend the next three hours emptying. They talk, dial the music louder, and then sometimes more softly, and talk and talk. After a time someone brings six more whiskey bottles to the table. They empty them all. I can't imagine how they actually walk away. And when they do, two stay behind, one yelling at the other while he pulls up the tablecloth and collects the empties. A bunch of bottle clustered by a table leg remain when the two men finally leave, with the loud man bellowing into the darkness as his companion shepherds him home.

It's fucking hot here without the rain or a breeze. I feel as if I'm sunburnt but I'm not. I am flushed as if I have a fever.

Wet clothes on a clothesline dry faster here than in Las Vegas in the summer.

Birds, bad music, the tractor bumbling along in the next field and the occasional sound of motorbikes on the road and the heat.

I've now slathered bug spray and hydrocortisone all over me ... feel pretty, pretty, pretty.

The next day, late afternoon, I walk into the village for medicine and find most of the main street battened down because of the afternoon heat. So I climb the stairs to a two story restaurant to get something to drink and eat at what is now our favorite diner in Sauhara. Across the street a fat guy sitting at his desk in a tourist shack nods off and catches himself. Some stores are empty because proprietors wander around when they've not got clients. A watchful neighbor will find them or show customers how to find them if necessary. I run into Sandy downstairs where the girl in coffee shop below the restaurant won't make a smoothie.

"I'm new," she said. "I don't know how."

So we headed home "smoothieless."

One growling dog drives another backwards until they suddenly stop and stand down. The kids start flowing down the street arm in arm, returning from school all dressed the same. Not just uniforms. Even the girls' hair is plaited the same and tied at the ends with the same bright green ties. A little boy, not quite 6, I'd bet, hands us his card "Tourist Service." He looks a little small for the job, but is mighty confident when I challenge his credentials. Sandy is entranced with the children. Goats left out to graze and dogs passing back and forth through traffic including one that has clearly been fed by tourists. It has learned a few tricks like delicately jumping up on the people who'll like it.

It was fantastic to talk to Sean today. I hadn't realized how much I miss him. He's in good humor given that he's six days into Ramadan. Of course, I caught him just as he was about to break his fast so his mood was on the upswing. He said that he's been driving the Syrians to the Mosque and breaking his fast there, but then gets trapped into 6 hours of prayer,

"Hard on the knees."

Back underneath our gazebo we sit by tall glasses of water and doze sitting upright. A trail of big black ants hustles across the center of our table. You get into bug watching here. The two German girls, across the table from me, are discussing bug progress. Where are they going? Why are they going just now? What do they want to get once they stopped going? Your mind dulls in the heat, but also, why not let the bugs have their fifteen minutes. Immediately after the sun sets the crickets start to sing and a rising wall comprised of a single tone overwhelms all the other sounds. A cricket chorus.

Sandy returns late. This time when she arrived at the elephant stable and found it empty she headed to the river hoping to find the handlers and the animals there. Instead of elephants she said she found a crowd of adults and children watching the sunset. Then she says that the children intrigued by a stranger clustered around her and demanded her attention for a while until their parents waved them off. Then a man set a folding chair on the ground and bid her to sit and talk to him. He said he was a Jewish businessman who regularly traveled in between Sauhara and Lumbini (birthplace of Buddha), as well as to the Himalayan foothills and beyond. He offered his services, I'm not certain what they were, but when Sandy turned him down he easily moved onto other topics. The villagers had seen Sandy walking the streets in the past week and wondered who she was and now took the opportunity to greet her and draw her into the conversation. It takes time to become part of the group in a small town, but these people easily included her although they knew she would only be passing through.

"We are local," one man said explaining how everyone knew everyone. She stayed as long as she could until just before it became too dark to safely cross the fields.

THE RIVER

Canoe trip today. Sandy didn't go because the jungle trek bored her. I know that all boats leak but it doesn't inspire confidence to see the owner bailing out his canoe before we board. "Wait please," he says until he is satisfied. Arjun, our innkeeper, joins me. He will take me to the elephant stables after the boat ride. We climb in and walk the length of boat that's a foot wide and 35 feet long and one of a dozen stacked up against one another. It isn't comfortable, but comfort is for sissys, I guess. Two guys (with gorgeous thighs and calves) shove us away from the shore with long bamboo poles. "Mind that your hands stay inside and please keep the boat balanced," one says. There are 3 tourist parties in the boat and so 3 competing narratives as the guides attempt to wow us. The sky is cloudy, but not threatening and I left my camera at home today because I don't want the distraction.

The bird song is thick and it drowns out the speakers. About half a dozen crocodiles doze in the water and we pass the half eaten corpse of a wild boar bobbing in the current. Small holes in the riverbank are bird lairs, smaller ones are for crabs and bigger ones are what the guides call crocodile palaces. It's time to lay eggs so the females crawl 10 meters onto the sandy areas to bury their offspring and, I guess, hope for the best. The locals are allowed to come into the park today and chop wood so we can hear axes ringing. One enterprising dude poles along the riverbank and collects logs that have fallen naturally.

"Do you want to walk through," Arjun says gesturing at a thick leafy stand of jungle growth. I just shake my head. He smiles. "Leeches not so bad here," he says.

Whatever.

After we get to shore he and I pursue a well-packed grassy path instead until we find a bridge and cross it back to the non-park side of the river. Then we trundle along the rocky paths that they call roads to the elephant birthing center. Used to be that the wild population was robust enough that it satisfied the human need to own elephants, but reduction in habitat and herd size necessitates breeding the elephants in a government run center. In the museum reception area a history of the place and the breeding process is presented in a poster-by-poster explanation, detailing the way the animals are trained and cared for. This lengthy presentation is accompanied by a list of diseases that kills elephants. Someone thought it was a good idea to hang a photograph of a baby elephant that had been born dead at the end of this list. And while the devices they use to control the animals are not torture tools, I just can't look at them all. It's pretty ugly. Outside the elephants are chained to posts underneath a high roofed enclosure. Several of the animals are exhibiting neurotic behaviors. As we walk away I see the handlers' quarters. They don't look more humane. "Women cannot because they are not strong enough to handle the elephant," the guide says. I buy an ice cream and a lemon Fanta because I suddenly need a heavy dose of sugar. Then the guide, the driver and I stuff ourselves back into the three wheeled motorized scooter we've been tooling around in and we are off to the elephant stable to participate in elephant bathing.

Sandy, of course, was already there preparing food.

Two elephants return to the stable within the hour. The handlers remove the elephants' saddles. Then the youngest handler yells at the bigger beast telling it to stand still while he climbs aboard. Arjun, Sandy and I walk alongside until we reach the grassland. There, just as we leave the road, Sandy and I climb aboard too and we head for the river with me perched on the animal's giant shifting shoulders, wondering when I'm falling off. Arjun follows us in order to take pictures. I have had enough of being Chitwan's favorite food source (I am peppered with bug bites) so I keep my pants on when we enter the river. Last night was fucking horrible. I have bites from my feet to my ass on both sides with clusters on both knees.

"There are leeches in the river," Arjun yells. There aren't, but from now on that's everyone's funny joke for me.

It's fun, but we are not providing a service. This is a tourist gig. We ride the beast into the river where she sprays herself according to her handler's instructions. Instructions are barked and for the most part she obeys pretty quickly. The water is cold enough to cut through the monsoon heat and she's got a powerful natural sprayer. Then she drops down, and rolls to her side the way moving mountaintops do. We dismount as she rolls because it's bad to be crushed like a wet twig. Eventually she lies on her side with her head submerged and her trunk poking above the water's surface like a natural snorkel. We dismount and scrub her with rocks. She's a redhead with a hide tougher than asphalt. It's like scraping the highway. The process is repeated several times, the spraying, the rolling and the scraping until we are done. Then the young elephant handler is paid and we part ways. Sandy and I are soaked but the sun will dry us in the time it takes us to walk back to the inn. There's no rain today so it's all heat and I would return the river alone just to cool down, but crocodiles live in the river and only the presence of the elephants protects us.

"God as separate from nature is a diseased idea. If you think of us as coming out of the earth rather than being cast down on it then we are the earth."

(Joseph Campbell, *The Power of Myth*).

LUMBINI

FACEBOOK POSTING MAY 24

You haven't lived until you've straddled the back of a motorcycle, while the Nepalese madman at the helm cheerfully weaves through traffic in which the drivers display what can only be called a casual idea of lanes and flow. I keep my eyes open because it's how I keep balance. He drives and I don't tip us over and I don't scream out loud while he veers back and forth into oncoming traffic. Buses and trucks blurt black smoke at us and the dust is high and in our faces, but there's a nice breeze which soothes me while we face down another city bus or semi that moves out of our way just in time.

How did I get here? Yesterday, a sign on a taxi in Chitwan advertising _Temple City in Lumbini!_ where Buddha was born, made me curious. Four hours in a bus, on mountain roads--again. Bought the ticket at a bus stand where a goat sits next to me on the bench in the waiting area. The bus conductor, who forces me into the correct seat, is a kid who checks tickets and decides when the bus should stop for passengers who stand at no particular place in the road. He bangs on the bus to make it stop and go. He's making his quota. The bus is jam-packed. He jumps on and off the bus while it's moving. He climbs up the side of the bus and walks up top while it's moving. He almost steps on my fingers once because he uses my window frame to lower himself. Whenever the bus stops vendors come and raise baskets of food and water to the windows. Everyone but me knows the prices. The girl next to me buys water and chips, and then tosses the empty bag out the window (I'M SITTING BY THE WINDOW). Then she takes a swig of water and leans across my lap and spits it out onto the road. She also offers me her water because I don't have any, so ...

I read detective novels and pass in and out of consciousness. I disembark at the wrong place which is a drag because someone was supposed to meet me at the right place so now I'm standing in downtown Lumbini breathing soot and heating up while I watch the cars and motorbikes play death race. I have a phone number and an address for tonight, but no telephone. Taxi drivers noticing my confusion converge. "Ride Madam?" "Ride Madam?" "Ride Madam?" "Ride Madam?" First of all STOP CALLING ME THAT. Secondly, they're really aggressive. "Ride Madam" sounds more like, "*Get in, Bitch.*"

I pick a guy. "How much?"

"1000 rupees."

"800."

"Yes."

That number will become 3500. After calling the hotel the driver says that he should drive me to the sites before taking me to my hotel because it is behind us. "When did it get behind us? Is it ambulatory?"

So now I commence on a tour of the Buddhist monuments, which is cool, I dig Buddha, but I also see a dearth of ladies in the creationist mythology. Fellas, she's missing except for when she can crouch down and give you a messiah or stretch out on a couch and help you make one. I love the Chinese temple. It has a PA system of metal daisies lining the walkways through which a man chants sutras designed to bless pilgrims but because of the system tonality it sounds like the dude is about to come after your 'nads instead. Oh, I haven't had anything to drink or eat since this morning. There's no real reason for this.

You have to walk barefoot in the temple areas but it's now 3 p.m. The ground has been sucking up heat since sunrise. At the first temple I am charmed by three girls in saris making the traditional clockwise circuit. They are running, as in filled with joy running. But when I step on the hot bricks that stand between me and holiness I realize that the girls are running because the bricks are searing hot. The bricks closer to the monuments are shaded, but you still have to bolt past the Dantean portion of the excursion to achieve mindfulness. I take my socks and shoes off and hurry across the porch to the stupa steps make my circuit and then dash back to my shoes. Ten temples. 20 mad dashes. Someone's gotta be laughing.

Where the fuck are my reading glasses? Oh hell. This is what necessitated the motorcycle chase because we are hunting down the taxi that has them. It's 7. p.m. Where is anything to eat or drink? Also I gotta wee.

NEXT MORNING IN LUMBINI

A sane person would stow everything in the same place every time when they traveled. But I am not she. I always have to urgently rummage through my whole pack to find that essential item that I have carelessly squirreled away. I always need the thing, the plug, the passport, the ticket, my glasses, the medicine, *now* and I'm usually in a public place like on the side of the road, or in front of a government official with twenty people standing in line behind me, looking like a demented Sadhu because I usually start tossing things around.

I've lost my glasses again.

Just being American means people want to take selfies with you. You're like a sea creature no one sees on land so when they catch you they need proof. Picture takers used to just point at their cameras and then at me, but now they all know the word "Selfie." Another gift from America. A friendly Indian mob cornered me just outside of Buddha's birthplace. There's a piece of rock inside that is the designated plop spot (exactly where he was born), par for the course with religious sites. There are also about ten thousand teeth of Buddha (the equivalent of slivers from the cross) for sale on this continent. And in Jerusalem there are dozens of places where Mary slept on that auspicious night.

But. Eeeeew.

Anyway, as I sit down outside the monument to put my shoes on AGAIN and repack my back pack (found my glasses in the shoes) when shadows move in and I realize that I am surrounded by Indians who want to take a picture with me. The Indian head bob gives them away. Not to diminish the bob, it's the catchall expression of "I mean to say whatever doesn't piss you off." It's great.

Back at the hotel I try to ensure that I will catch my return bus to Chitwan by discussing the matter with the staff because nothing works like clockwork here. I give up dinner for this. No matter,

I'd eaten a whole apple this morning.

"I want to return to Chitwan tomorrow."

My motorcycle guy waves away my concerns about finding the bus stop on my own. "I will drive something, something, something," he says to me.

"You will drive me to the bus stop?" I'm using hand gestures that mean nothing.

"Yes. Yes." He nods confidently.

"I will get there in time to take the 9 a.m. bus?"

"Yes. Sure."

The next morning he is a no show. While drinking coffee, which I have to insist should have no cream or sugar in it or it comes to me as thick as chocolate milk, I notice that the hotel clock is thirty minutes faster than mine. I'm up too late. I ask two members of the hotel staff, who don't speak English very well, for help. It's the way they emphasize syllables that makes the English they do speak hard to understand and I don't speak Nepalese at all so .... After ten minutes, they decide to bring in a guy from the kitchen who speaks less English than they do. He and I point at stuff and hope the other one "gets it" until someone else calls a telephone number I have written on a *Hotel Park Inn* card Arjun gave me before I left Chitwan.

"This," says the desk clerk. After hanging up the phone, he and his friend point at the card I gave them earlier. "They will leave five hours from now." Hand wave as if this idea is insane. You can take "buetter" bus, much "buetter."

"A bus to Chitwan?" I say. They all nod. The very idea is exciting.

I choose to believe that they agree that the better bus will get me there, but it's just as likely that they are just agreeing that's what I said. I suspect that I paid for a round trip ticket yesterday, but I'd rather go now. So I climb back onto the death mobile and we race off to the bus station.

"Chitwan. Chitwan National Park?" I say to the ticket sellers. Three fat dudes sitting behind wire mesh are enjoying their mid-morning meal.

"Sauhara!" they respond.

"Yea, sure," I say meaning if you even get me anywhere near my desired destination I can walk or hire myself out to pick mangos for the season or make elephant bricks. I'm getting good at that.

My Nepalese Mad Max asks the men questions and agrees to wait with me to ensure that I get on the bus that could be heading near, but not exactly where I want to go.

"Chitwan. Sauhara?" I asked the conductor as I climb onto a bus with small metal seats.

He nods. "Sure." I keep my backpack with me in case I see that we have driven into India or Sri Lanka by mistake and I need to crawl out the window.

The man who sits next to me sits half in my lap. Wherever we touch, legs, arms, waistlines, we sweat. The bus rocks and rolls and rockets off pot holes so hard that we bounce off our seats and everyone grabs the handles on the seat in front of them at the same time. The bus driver is honking like crazy which means "I am heading directly at you, what do you think?" Huge construction vehicles pass us on the right, inches away, bouncing when they hit pieces of broken pavement. I have to choose between inhaling the dust being kicked up by the traffic or suffering in a windless hot box with the window closed.

"Construction" the man next to me explains after donning a surgeon's mask. He has decided to explain many things to me. He's not speaking English, but clearly he's pointing things out to me and, you know, explaining.

When bus stops, for whatever reason, a vender, selling lychee nuts, jumps aboard. As the bus starts to roll, he leaps back onto the street hitting the pavement at a balanced run.

Three hours in, my friend (the explainer) and the conductor inform me that although we are in a place I do not recognize, I need to disembark.

"Chitwan?" They nod and point to taxis, open air motor scooters.

"Yes. Yes."

Yes, what the fuck do you mean, Yes?

I get out and wade into the taxi-man fray. They don't seem to know what I want until I find a soldier who points at a guy. I hand him a crumpled *Hotel Park Inn* card. He nods and quotes what would be an outrageous price, if I were spending real money.

Giving in, I nod. "But then you take me to my hotel door," I say.

"Yes, yes."

It's an open air cab and a pleasant ride. We reenter park territory. Open fields, lots of green and the return to the bloodsuckers that all know my name. It's like that moment in *Cry the Beloved Country* when the priest returns and the villagers start singing. Except for me they're singing, "She's here. She's here, line the fuck up and finish her off." My feet are covered in scabs.

The driver passes my hotel. I've been daydreaming so I miss it too, but I do notice that we are "home" so I pay and jump out. I haven't eaten yet today. The only thing I've swallowed is a cup of instant coffee, so I find a restaurant in Chitwan that serves "American" food. I need the fiber and some fresh fruit. They've been loading me up with rice and my body is not pleased. I order a cheese burrito, iced coffee, water, and fruit juice and start writing. I try to use the toilet but its dark and smelly in there, so I change my mind but I can't go back to my room yet. I don't want to sit inside. Then I see Sandy and she joins me. She needs a juice. When she tries to pay she is told that a girl sitting at another table has paid her tab and gone. We remember a group of

53

six young women and men, a quiet group that sat on the other side of the restaurant for a while. It's a riddle. Then Sandy convinces me to accompany her to the elephant stables and I forget about who paid for what, but I know that Sandy will obsess about it until she's repaid the favor.

When we arrive at the stables only the children are there, waiting for Sandy who played football with them yesterday. Today she hands out pretty blue and pink plastic vials of soapy water with bubble wands attached which attracts every child the village. The toys are cheap and some of the tops break off so that they can't be opened, but she still has enough for all including the youngest who tries to drink then eat his. Six of the kids lead us to the back of their home, a moldy crumbling structure where they offer us different kinds of fruit from their trees and decide against playing football. When we return to the stable we find one of the handlers hiding out. He gets us started preparing food. My fingers have increased tensile strength at this point. Like a flock of geese, the kids gather around and watch. I can't imagine why this interests them. Until I hear the whispers. They want candy. We are the source. Also they have questions.

"How many children do you have?" It is expected that there are children.

"Three," I say. Three dogs and three cats but why quibble.

"Where is your husband?" they ask as I fold a thick stalk of hay into a square dish shape.

"I don't know. Do you?" I pour rice in the hay bowl I've made and the force the hay around it so that I can bind it altogether with another stalk of hay.

They giggle because it's an insane reply. "Is he a good husband?"

"Eh." I say. They gasp. "He is at home watching our babies."

A tap at my elbow. "I like your tattoos. GRRRR." That is Unita and she is prettier than any other child I have ever seen. The kids love my lion tattoo.

Once the elephants return we wash them, which today entails pumping water into a bucket or directly into the elephants' trunks so they can spray themselves which they do and if not to their owner's satisfaction, he orders them to wash again. Afterwards more food making. Then the animals are chained up and fed. This process can take up to an hour. I sense that it's essential that they eat and that you cannot leave them alone with food and assume they will eat enough. The handlers watch closely. When an animal ignores its food they order it to eat. Then it either takes a bundle from our hands or picks it off the ground and touches and tests it. It uses its trunk to feel around the edges, rolls it around like a kid playing with its food and then finally it stuffs the morsel; deep into its mouth and you see a stretch of tongue that is impossibly huge. Its teeth seem to be far back in its mouth and you hear a satisfying solid grinding sound that makes you want to try eating the stuff yourself. They eat slowly and if the hay packet unrolls in their mouths they reject it. They pull the straw out and toss it behind them. It's a gentle gathering moment at the end of the day. The kids are still with us because we're new to them, but I think that the whole family starts to drift together at this time of day. Kids that are too young to work yet, watch while their parents attend to their evening chores everyone moving within talking distance of one another while the oldest men sit and smoke.

MORNING: BACK AT THE PARK

Hotel Park Inn has been invaded by a troop of Indians. They arrived yesterday via an ultra luxurious bus but today is when they make their presence felt. They settle into their rooms with a lot of chatter and fanfare while someone sets up a camping kitchen on the driveway. They have brought all their own food and pots and pans. Walking past the rooms now requires a ton of Namastes and a question or two. "Where are you from?", "How long is your trip?", "Been to the jungle?", "Have you been to Calcutta yet? You must."

Brightly colored clothing and luggage is unloaded and unpacked, lots of kids racing up and downstairs, laundry festooning the railings and a sense that we are now a guest in someone else's housing complex. The children run easily from room to room, dressed or not. The women sit in pairs in the mornings and talk while the men smoke and talk. Everyone yells to one another from one side of the building to the other. The children in particular don't need to be anywhere near their parents when they address them.

"Hello," a man calls to me from up on the first floor. I look up to see his whole family at the railing smiling down at me.

"Good morning!!!" he says. And then, they all wave at me.

"Hey, folks!" I reply. They smile and wave at me again like they're on a ship leaving port. Jenny the dog barks at people selectively. She simply doesn't care for some people. From time to time women come to the railings and turn clothing over that they washed as soon as they got off the bus yesterday. It will dry if the sun hits it. If not it can take up to two days to dry completely.

It rains in the night. The hours before a storm are miserable. The air super heats and becomes very humid until you don't know how you can stand it but then you hear thunder and you know respite is on the way. When the rain finally comes and the temperature drops and the dogs bark because they hate lightening. The wind tears off loose pieces of buildings and flings them into the yard. But the next morning is a cool beginning and everyone is energized and they take advantage of it because the heat will return.

Sandy and I settle down for breakfast but it takes a while. A pair of Indian women standing on the walk, not ten feet away, watch us. They talk and stare and then finally join us. Two more women also dressed in magenta, orange and bright yellow saris quickly follow them. Each wears two or three thick gold bracelets their wrists, gold earrings and nose clips. It seems like a lot of maintenance to me. We cross the language barrier with repetition, hand gestures and iPhones. The women pass around ours around and nod and smile and talk among themselves. They are here for two days only, that much we understand. Then they thank us and leave and soon after another group joins us: three men and an older woman with no teeth. Sorry, but that's the detail that stands out. They want selfies. Several different groups come now to take pictures of selfies with us until that's done, then they thank us and leave.

It's still early morning when the birds are most active. Clicking, chirping, bleeping, hooting and screeching. It is soothing to watch them bounce from the trees to the grass to the straw topped gazeboes while we eat. Gecko's crawling around the bamboo beams and make the usual clicking sounds. The bigger ones chase the smaller ones away. No one is working in the fields today.

Sandy leaves to prepare to go to "my elephants" early. She also has tasked herself with playing football with the children and giving more toys (more vials of soapy water with bubble wands attached) to those who missed out yesterday.

I follow after a bit and we spend the entire morning traipsing between the stables and the river elephants. The first time we arrive at the stable children burst forth. They lure us inside and one bounces on a bed (wooden plank lifted off the ground by a few feet). A man groans and one of the handlers hidden under a blanket, stirs so Sandy and I keep walking all the way through to the back door. The kids pester Sandy if their toys have run out of liquid. Unita Kumar the littlest girl and the youngest boy are still entranced. The boy's refilled his with water and has discovered that this is a no go. The older children, however, sing a different tune. "Candy? Money?" And now they want to play football, which doesn't interest Unita who stands on the field for five minutes ducking and wincing before retreating to safety. Today they discover our iPhones and scroll through our pictures while Sandy and I "work". They're not impressed by how many dog pictures I have, but they dig all the family stuff. For simplicity's sake I lie about who is who. "Yes, those are my children." I have no human children.

"Friend." Anyone who doesn't fit into the other categories.

"Husband." Two of those.

"Yes, Grandmother." I don't know who that is a picture of, but now I'm on a roll creating a whole cast of family members that I don't have. Sandy shovels elephant shit and we "make food" until it dawns on us that maybe the handlers have gone straight to the river. So off we go.

Left. Left. Stay on the left side of the road.

At the river a gaggle of bone thin boys and girls use the bridge as a diving board. Two women take their babies into the water and wash them and their long black hair. One then leaves but the water is pleasantly chilling and after a time the woman who stays floats on her back while a boy takes command of the baby. A man in a fishing hat standing midstream drags a net through the water. Then he collects something (eels and tiny fish, it turns out) out of it and puts it in a basket attached to his belt.

"Aren't you afraid of crocodiles," I ask him standing safely on shore.

"No, no. The river's not high enough. When it rains," he makes a sweeping gesture. "Many come, but not now. Do you want to try?" He indicates with his fishing net. I join him and his wife who is nearby collecting grass off the river bottom for her ducks. "I was a guide," he replies when I ask. "But too dangerous. Rhinos with babies, tigers and bear." He shakes his head. "No, too dangerous. I do official documents now." Then he shows me the proper technique for dredging eels out of the water. He is going to make eel soup, I think. His words are a stew of Nepali and

English. He has that gut that half the men get here. Some stay rail thin forever. Since whatever these men do for a living here they all live a physically laborious life. I don't know how anyone gets fat.

"I live just there." The fisherman points to a straw and clay construct to our right. "You must come for dinner. I will show you how to cook these." And he shows me his catch so far. It's a slimy mix. His house is just next to a posh resort, which reminds me of beach clubs in Southern California. Brick riverfront, gazebos and lounge chairs by the river and a brightly colored well tended, though presently unpopulated, clubhouse. I promise nothing, but I'll keep the offer in mind. It's not that I don't want to go, it's that I'm not up to planning. The heat and the easy pace of this place has turned me into a bit of a drifter despite my Germanic tendencies.

"The head is not where consciousness originates. It inflects consciousness in a certain direction. Consciousness and energy are the same things. So consciousness is life, the energy of the universe, the mind orders and directs it."

(Joseph Campbell, *The Power of Myth*)

A LITTLE VISITOR

"Morning" A beautiful little girl has found me after I sit down to write. I have to look around. She is standing in the unfinished window frame on the second story of the unfinished building next door. She's fairy tale pretty.

"Morning?" I think it may be the only English she knows because its 3 p.m.

"Who are you?"

"Morning?" She smiles and waves to me. I smile, wave back and returned to my writing.

"Morning?" Now she's on the ground floor peering at me through another window frame. She smiles. Maybe six, pigtails tied with the ubiquitous green silk ribbon. Green t-shirt with a teddy bear insignia and a full set of teeth when she smiles. She points at me whenever I ask another question and then disappears. I keep writing.

"Hello?" Now she's just on the other side of the barbed wire fence from me.

"Who are you?"

"Hello?"

"How are you?"

She smiles and laughs and runs away. Back to the computer.

"Morning?" She's back upstairs. I feign shock. Then she shows me that she has a silver coin which she palms just before she disappears from view. She reappears on the ground again. We play pantomime for a while until we finally get to the crux of our conversation.

"Money?" she says as she holds her very cute hand out to me.

I stay under the gazebo writing for some time. Enough time for the owner's young son, Adam, to find me and appropriate my computer for a movie, two games and several YouTube moments. The little girl who wanted money returns with a friend and together they chant "Money?" at me for a while. Then I see a swatch of color through the bushes, which must be Sandy's pants coming up the walk. Once she clears the bushes I see she has company. Two girls, late teens, early twenties. Bright, fresh faced, and very enthusiastic Americans. One says she's from Chicago and the other is from Orange County in California. Sandy leads them up the walk because, "They wanted to meet you." She met them on her search to find the mystery women who had paid for her drink and it turns out to be one of these girls. They are staying at the posh place across the river. We talk a little. At the very end of the conversation one of them says that she'll "pray on it" in response to some problem we discuss and I have this sense that these girls being very careful about what they say. Then all three leave and apparently the girls part ways with Sandy down the road. "They have Bible study from 6-10 at night," Sandy explains." And there we have it. The drink was a way to meet Sandy and perhaps bring her to the light by inviting her to Bible study. Creepy Christians everywhere you look. No direct statements, just subterfuge.

Lemme see. Something buggy and big bit my leg just as I was turning in. Also the Indians have gone, but a Nepalese group has moved in and these motherfuckers drink and just won't go to bed. Because the owners of this place don't bring Jenny in at night and because at night she barks at everyone who moves about (and who won't fucking go to bed) I can't sleep. It calms me a little when I go outside, where *the rest* of the mosquitoes await, but it's not like I'm sleeping. I can't just put earbuds in and turn the music up loud because I will still know that the dog is upset. Jesus! Also it's hotter inside than outside in part because Sandy does not like to open the windows even if there are screens so the breeze can only come in from my side of the room and you need you know, fucking flow. She doesn't like to feel air moving about so she also doesn't like the fan going which is happening anyway because even she can't stand how hot it gets when the fan is still. So now I'm outside because the dog calms down when she sees me. Someone is snoring so loud that it sounds like a dog growling. Fuckers. Fuckers. Fuckers. GO TO SLEEP. And then they turn the router off so I can't even harass Sean or watch a movie off the Internet.

If you walk back and forth through Chitwan for a week, even if you only travel through the tourist areas, eventually everyone seems to know you and you know most everyone after a fashion. I wander through the village in the afternoon. There's the old lady with the scrunched face who never straightens up when she walks. She smirks at me when she sees me. She's always dressed in green, green sari or a green towel wrapped around her body as she gingerly picks her way back from the shower which is a makeshift stall behind the house. I've learned after a week of "Namastes," that she doesn't hate me, that's just her face. There's the kid, (five or less year old) who was brandishing a razor blade yesterday while his mother sat nearby. He likes sharp objects and she doesn't leave him unattended. There are six old men who sit on the same bench like monkeys where the road is sheltered by a stand of trees talking in low tones to one another all day long. There are mothers squatting on steps just inside the doorways grinding rice with Stone Age tools while they mind the family stall, many of which are unattended now in the bitchy, blistering early afternoon heat. Tourists are hiding in their rooms. Locals are quietly waiting and watching for sunset and the rise of the bugs. When I pass a field and I hear high-pitched growls and turn to see six kids with scrunched faces holding their hands as if they had claws. They are half a block behind me. If they know your name they call it but if they don't they give you a nickname. You could be Sandy's friend (because they can remember Sandy), Bigger (because you carried a big bottle of water), Football (because you played it or held one or maybe even sat on one and rolled off it). In my case, GRRRR because of the tattoo of a lion I have on my arm. The Chitwan consensus is that it's the best of all my tattoos. A little boy saw it and growled and so now that's my name. Six kids catch up to me all growling. I growl back as is the custom. They are returning from school. The crowd envelops me.

"Remember me?" The tallest and oldest of this group. Another totally confident child.

"Yes, I say, football." We've played it a few times now. I am remembering the good old days and am therefore cementing our long association.

"Yeeeeess," he says speaking to me like a child who has finally, finally figured out how to spell "cat." "Candy? Money? Coca-Cola?" A focused individual, not into subterfuge.

I shake my head. "Not until the last day" I lie. Maybe, maybe not. I'll do my best.

A frown. "The last day," he says, sealing the deal. The children keep me surrounded as we walk. I have midget protection. Then from across a green field (about half a block wide) more yelling and six more kids burst through what you could call hedges and race to join us as if I was about to disappear. "They've bagged a tourist! Come quickly!" The same questions are repeated and others are posed that I don't understand. No one seems to care. I have to provide the names of the tourists who will show up at the stable tonight, then say when I am returning and then I need to explain why I will come tomorrow instead of tonight and then, I must reaffirm my promise. "Last day," the oldest boy says.

This happens in the space of ten minutes then everyone scatters. I keep walking. I have about half a mile of heat to endure before I get home where I will shed my clothes and sit and sweat while I try to get the words down. Can you be allergic to heat? My skin feels prickly.

The clouds move in so thickly and swiftly that they bring night-time on earlier than usual. Then the lightning strikes begin. It seems as if there are dozens of strikes at once. Electricity leaps from the ground like a hoard of fireflies. It seems like there are three sources of lightening. The lightening is silent and only the brightest ones show up on video. Fairies in the storm. The air smells like elephant poop, which isn't a bad thing. Elephant poop smells like hay and soil. Sandy and I caught out in the open, in the sudden rainstorm, run to a common indoor dining room that we have never used and find that the door is stuck. The men, rushing in behind us, pound on it to get it open. Jenny is already inside. She sits next to me for a bit. Adam comes in carrying his baby sister. Dinner is water and a plateful of noodles. Geckos crawl overhead while the rain beats down on corrugated metal. After a while we open the windows taking advantage of the cold wind and sit for a couple of hours just listening to the rain.

The crickets start singing when the rain stops.

I will not be walking into the jungle tomorrow. I will take a jeep. Sandy is going to pass altogether.

There are two other girls at the table when I meet up with Sandy for lunch. They've already gotten their food but lunch is at least a three hour affair here. It couldn't possibly matter that I still need to order. This place has incredible Wi-Fi. Journalists and web masters come here when they need a reliable Internet connection. Of course I will be changing all my passwords when I get back home because all the connections here are not secure.

The girls are chronologically in their early twenties, but person-ality-wise, think early teens. Think Malibu Barbie's younger sister, Skipper.

"We've been traveling to poor countries the last six months," the one with the pixie hair cut says. She bought Sandy's drink. I still don't know why and the way she says poor countries makes me think she means underprivileged and heathen.

"They want to know about living in Los Angeles," Sandy says to me. I say that I haven't lived there in a decade, but okay.

"Where is the best place to live in Los Angeles, cheaply," the blond asks. "We'll be waitressing." On waitress salary, how about in a box underneath the 405, I think TO MYSELF as I sketch out the basics.

They smile and smile and smile. I try not to sneer because we need some balance. Pixie wears an orange baseball cap that says "His Blood Matters." They are so fresh faced that it hurts to look at them. There's no need to learn their names, as individuals they are interchangeable. I can't put my finger on it, but they creep me out and I feel as if I am being pumped for information although I have none, of any consequence, and I wonder why I feel this way because the girls just asking questions anyone does when you start up a conversation. There is talk of contracts by which they mean promising on paper not to have sex until marriage, which wouldn't be creepy either, necessarily, but these two seem wonky. (God why would you, I think TO MYSELF)

"What do you believe?" Pixie asks me three and a half hours in. And when I tell her she hooks onto the word truth. "What is the truth?" and it's the tone, not the question. She's sure I can't get to a concrete answer. Whatever I say next stops her from continuing that line of thought. The girls invite Sandy who is closer to their age, to come to dinner and meet the rest of their group. They are staying at the posh place across the river. I don't see her again until eleven that night. I am worried that they will unearth some intense religiosity in Sandy because that would ruin our, thus far, easygoing relationship. We consider ourselves lucky that we get along so well.

She returns home later than ever before.

"It was all very nice," she says. "But there was too much talk of Jesus."

And then the good news. "They are leaving tomorrow."

Back into the jungle after elephant baths tomorrow.

ELEPHANT BATH TWO

Pro Tip: You can fall off an elephant and she can shake you off her back like a weak flea and fling you into the river whenever she wants. I drank a lot of river water today.

They've told me the elephants' names but I can't remember them. I can't make sense of Nepalese. It's not like these girls will come running if I call them by name anyway.

We wash the older elephant in the river in the morning and then pump water for her so that she can spray herself in the evening. I work the pump and try to keep the water flowing so that whenever she's ready she only has to hold her trunk out to be filled. Then she raises her trunk and sprays a massive amount of water on herself drenching me in the process as well. In the photographs the water can look like a spinning ever widening circle of wet when she shoots it out.

The older elephant is a beautiful girl and she does what she's told and I'm thrilled to be so close to her and to be interacting with her but I wonder about her life. The younger elephant stays tied up when Sandy and I are around. The Nepalese say that she's prone to acting out. She is at first the more overtly interactive of the two, which makes me like the older one better. Whenever we pay too much attention to the younger one the older animal reaches over and yanks the youngster's ear. (Youngster is 25 years old.)

Trunk tips are like very strong very dexterous fingers and it's amazing to hand food to them and to feel them search your pockets for goodies. You feel like you've won a prize when they take something from you. Sandy finds an itchy spot on the younger one's stomach. When the animal decides that it is time for Sandy to scratch her on the other side of her stomach she picks her up and moves her to that side so quickly that I almost wondered if I'd seen it happen. The handlers chastise her after the fact. I can't tell if the animal gives a damn. I do see that she stands still so Sandy can continue to scratch.

Their size forces them to move gracefully. They don't lumber, they glide. They kneel and stand very slowly. They move as if they have great patience and all the time in the world and then they can move very quickly and remind you of their monumental strength of which we will only see a portion. There is some talk of some handlers being hurt. The early days training for elephants is ugly and meant to break the animals' spirits. There is nothing to stop these guys from being cruel and elephants do not forget, but on the whole no one who lives with these beasts is scared of them. Several times we are warned against approaching them if the handlers are not present. They are treated well-ish, in part because they are income and unhappy beasts get sick and cannot be trusted around tourists, and they cannot be easily replaced. Only the government may breed them and I don't know what you need to do to get a permit to own one.

I've been taking pictures of the animals in pieces as well as of the whole animals. I am reminded of the joke about the 3 blind men who only know the part of the elephant they are touching. Craggy, creased, grey, soft, abrasive, gentle, big, balanced, elegant, as strong as fuck, entrancing. They live for decades. They can outlive their handlers. They look like they've seen everything. They have complex relationships with one another in the wild. I can only imagine what must go on in their heads.

Sandy and I brought all our photo gear to the river and to the stables today. We easily take 100s of shots of one another and lots of video, which we send to each other's accounts after looking them over. The handler is touching Sandy's, hair in a number of them, something she hadn't been aware of at the time.

MONSOON

The storms always come the same way. It suddenly gets very, very hot in a place that is always dry and hot. It's like feeling a battery charge. Then the humidity ramps up. A wall of wet hits you. You think you have about four hours of daylight left, but instantly you have none. The sky turns dark grey and suddenly you are traveling in nighttime. Then the thunder starts which means in twenty minutes the rain will come.

I chose the jeep excursion today because it has been raining and I just don't want to pick leeches out of my socks anymore. We've seen rhino, deer, boar, a sloth bear, monkeys, peacocks and crocodiles so far. Looking for tigers now. We've heard the deer bark, usually a warning to the others that there's a big cat nearby. So we're waiting here 19 Km from the river that surrounds the park.

When I feel a few raindrops on my face, I stuff my camera and phone in plastic bags and put my eyeglasses away so that I only have to concern myself with my backpack if we have to run. I don't have a rain jacket because it disappeared from my room last night. The guide looks up and tells the driver to start the jeep. We are done hunting tigers. We are speeding. I grab the back of my seat. The dark sky and the thick foliage suck up the light. The headlights are useless. I can't imagine how the driver can see. We are in a hurry, but the "road" is a rocky trough gutted with muddy depressions and the bridges we cross are homespun structures that need to be gingerly addressed unless you want to roll the jeep. Also, you can rock passengers out of these open vehicles.

The wind blows horizontally. If you have a hat it's gone. Sticks, pebbles, pieces of plant, sand and anything small enough is being driven into us and around us. I hold up my hands to protect my face. The 8 foot high elephant grass beats us as we pass through. We would like to get to the river before the rains really come or the current will be too rough and we'll have to wait. It may already be too late because the wind kicks it up a couple of notches every few minutes. It seems to get darker and windier still until finally the rain unleashes in sheets as we pull into the clearing where we intend to park. Four other vehicles are there and they're empty so maybe the other groups made it back in time. "Too late to cross," the guide shouts, so we are shepherded under two small lean-tos that don't begin to cover us all. They tilt so low on one side that those up front, me and another woman, must squat and try to keep off the ground which is puddling up. We try to keep as far underneath the protection as we can, but the water from the roof drains inward onto us. Those who can't fit are huddling under a hand held tarp. The rain lasted for 3 hours last night. Trees, weeds and grass bend and anything lightweight has taken flight and is pelting us and the jeeps.

Two dozen soggy trekkers returning from the river, join us. They're soaked and cold. Just 40 minutes ago it was effing hot and the jungle was filled with the sound of crickets so loud that they drowned out everything else, now it's all wind and water. After an hour of this the guide says he has plastic bags for our stuff if we want to try the river in the storm. Most of us agree and everyone runs which is a mistake, because the ground is slick. At the river two boatmen on the other side are bailing with coffee cans. One group waits ahead of us and 15 more people, the ones who didn't want to come, have followed in a straggling fashion. The first boatman poles over. The waves are rolling the boats which sit about 5 inches above the water's surface. The first load of passengers, which doesn't include my crowd, climbs aboard. There's a little jostling as some are more anxious than they have to be in my opinion, but I get it. I feel fully capable of shoving whomever I need to into the river. But we're not clinging to the railing on the Titanic. We are just uncomfortable. The only real danger is if we overturn the boat. We settle 18 people a piece into these slender vessels and the men poling try to keep the boats from swinging sideways to the current. As we near the other shore and just before we land I see, three feet from my hand, a caramel colored head and crocodile eyes. I see the full length of its body before it closes its eyes and drops beneath the surface. Then our boat hits the other shore and we disembark. The instant we do the rain stops.

ELEPHANT STABLE

"I hate this," I've rolled down my socks so I can scratch my ankles. "Socks catch bugs, make me hot and make my feet itch."

I still can't make the move to flip-flops (because feet are fucking ugly), but I am walking around in sockless running shoes.

Sandy has been walking around in crocs the entire time. "You've been here for weeks and now, only in the last days, you learn," she replies.

We step in, around, through and over obstacles as we make our way to the stable. Loose boarders separate one field from the next, both animals and people freely cross these. But it is as if the fences are indications rather than solid boundaries.

The elephants have not returned from the jungle treks when we arrive at the stable. The doors are closed, but Sandy is intent on making food anyway. She'll work in the stall out back but I want to write. I risked bringing the laptop tonight. When the animals return, they'll get washed down here at the pump and then get shackled and fed. I will help once they get here, but I'm done with brick making. Sandy has impressed the men with her discipline of making food.

Two men appear, the one with a crush on Sandy and his elder. The older man strips to the waist and washes himself at the pump. Despite warnings the younger man has attempted to kiss Sandy and definitely has a thing about touching her hair. It's par for the course in a country where blonds and red heads are nonexistent. Then the men open the stable doors and add to Sandy's provisions while I sit down to write. No one understands this habit, but I'm a tourist so I'm allowed to be odd.

Not enough has been said about the goats. They pepper the landscape. Every family has at least one. This is the time of year when corn is being harvested by hand. Left over plant parts are quickly collected up, particularly now that the rains have started, because the plant matter rots quickly and if you collect it before that happens you can feed it to the elephants and the goats, who love corn husks and stalks. The men at the stable shoo the goats away from their growing pile but three of the beasts, two coffee colored females and a black youngster whose ears flop when she runs, are particularly focused on the prize. The minute the men turn away the brown goats return. The black one hangs back hiding behind a brick wall until she is sure that it's safe. Then she returns and all three bite and gulp as fast as they can because they know time is short.

Only the oldest child, Ayus (12), is here so far. He tries to tell me how to spell his name and I get it wrong again and again until he gives up and types it in himself. He's old enough to be in charge and therefore is more serious than the others in some ways. It's hard to describe the relationships between the children here. There is a definite pecking order but these children are intimately connected. They move together and they share toys and food automatically. One is responsible for the other. Whenever any of them cannot explain themselves to me because of the language barrier another shows up, as if by design, to fill in the words. They seem kinder to one another than I remember being as a child, but then I am an outsider. What do I know? It must be there but I don't see the anger that flares up from time to time in groups of kids I know at home.

Since both men are out of bed by now, I duck inside the shed to sit on one of the cots and write down the details while I have my computer with me. Part brick and part wood, the shed is a very solid structure that houses three wooden cots and a huge rice bin, full at this point in the season. The well-swept brick and dirt floor seems cleaner than my kitchen at home. Clotheslines run along the back wall. All the handlers' belongings are kept in the stable. I think they live here during shifts. I can see the outhouse through the back door of the stable. It's a fragile structure, tilted like the Leaning Tower of Pisa. The walls sag, there is a hole cut into one side and a corrugated metal roof, laden with big chunks of cement, sinks in the middle. I'll hold it until we get back to our rooms and can use a proper bathroom.

Burlap bags, sacks of seed, a battered bicycle. Sandy sitting on the floor ignoring the straw pallet they offer to protect her from the floor. Two bags of elephant food (about 4 feet high) stuffed to the gills. A picture of Jesus on the cross bathed in a white halo hanging on the wall. It's Bubban's (the older handler), one I haven't met before who has now washed and dressed in a green t-shirt and khaki pants.

I don't want to know what is now feeding on my ankle. Whatever.

Bubban and Ayus are fascinated by the fact that they are being written about. Bubban sits cross-legged on his cot and stares at me while Ayus hovers over my shoulder as I write ... no pressure.

Everywhere here you can see evidence of nature resisting erasure. Overgrown and uncontained plant life. The fruit trees are laden. The locales will harvest as much as they can, but much will fall to the ground and be returned to the soil. I look up from my laptop. Two new visitors: one girl and one boy, attracted to the tourists. They insist that I add their name to my journal: Anis and Simon. The pack of coconut cookies I brought with me is instantly consumed. I have to cross the road and buy two more. And now the group grows. Three more children appear like fairies popping up out of the atmosphere. Tonight the girl Unita wears a flowered dress and flip-flops. Ayus sports a green tank top, a necklace with a Buddhist symbol, shorts and flip-flops. I am the only one here wearing long pants and closed toed shoes.

The back door faces west. The sunset spreads out over the sky spanning the horizon and changing the color of the landscape as the sun drops. The sky seems to reflect the color of the soil and takes on warm tones. The heat is backing off and it seems to me that everyone is almost done working. The pace is easy just now and the children who don't have chores or homework gather around the adults or sit in their laps. The women wrap their arms around the littlest ones as they talk to each other and the men explain what they are doing to the children who watch them as they work.

Ayus has taken control of my computer. I was typing his dictation but the going is slow. He says he has learned Word in school and suggests that he take over. I hand him the laptop and he types quickly as three younger boys crouch around him and watch the magic happen. They reach over his shoulder and touch the screen pointing out problems with the text. Fonts in particular fascinate them. When the computer is returned I have several files with the same words typed in BOLD, Italic, and underlined, blocked, capitalized and curly cued.

A second cluster of children have liberated Sandy's iPhone. She has given them specific instructions as to what they may do and they are scrupulously obeying her edicts. The children are young, but are also very respectful of private property. Unita and one of the littlest boys inform me that it is time to play. Her language skills improve once she separates from her brothers and she is a curious child. Using the tools at hand I teach her hopscotch, tiddlywinks and a weird form of marbles because we have to use rocks. Then we start playing Lion. I run after the little ones growling and at the end of the field they turn and chase me back across the field growling and baring their "claws." The game makes a stir and other children start to appear running out from their homes and climbing through the bushes and soon there are more than a dozen of us running back and forth across the field past the goats who are still working the corn stalk pile as the adults also come out to sit and talk and watch us play. I suspect that I look like an idiot.

Outside in the elephant stalls the big beasts rustle through the clean straw. Whenever they are taken out for a tourist jaunt, the men left behind shovel shit and replace dirty straw with new. The shit looks to be 90% processed hay. The men also have to regularly trim the elephants' toenails so I think cleanliness is meant to protect the human beings as well as the elephants.

A FEW THINGS:

1. Fuck socks. They're just bug catchers and they irritate the welts on my legs, feet, arms, back, stomach, hips, knees, ankles, shoulders, AND THE PALMS OF MY HANDS.

2. Send blood. I even have bug bites on the soles of my feet.

3. How can one sweat so much and not shrivel up like a raisin? Where is the liquid coming from?

4. No more rice. No more rice. No more rice ... please God.

5. Send coffee. This business of being automatically served only a demi-tasse of instant coffee is unacceptable. My body can't cope.

6. Please ... I DIDN'T VOTE FOR HIM.

7. The tip of an elephant's snout is good for stealing your iPhone out of your pocket. It's my fault, she was searching for mangoes. (Then you gotta catch it after she tosses it away.)

8. Watch where you step if elephant poop shoveling is still going on. You can end up in the big ditch where everyone is tossing the elephant poop. (It's a little on fire, by the way, because that's how they recycle it.)

9. Tigers and rhinos can cruise on by while you're sipping your morning cuppa. (I'm used to the elephants.) Do they prefer decaf or French Roast? I'm just gonna keep typing.

10. I really like it here.

WARNING ON A BUS.

Articles with Passengers are self responsible

From the, if only English were German collection.

RAFTING

I'm up early. I didn't sleep. A wave of free-floating anxieties about money and other obnoxious things kept me up. I have to be ready by 7:30am to catch the bus that will take me to the Trisuli River. I'm up at five and walk to the road in time to to see Arjun, his brother, and his nephew returning from a morning run. They ask me to join them as they sit down for a breakfast of hot tea and sea salt. The nephew has just returned from India and is heading to medical school. He wants to matriculate in America, because he wants to be surgeon and what do I know about qualifying for American medical programs? I am saved from looking stupid when Arjun notices the time and wonders where my bus is. Arjun and his brother have assured me that I will get a bus back to the Inn as well. Before I walk back to the road they check to see that I have money, a pack, water and someone hands me a telephone and the hotel card with several numbers on in case I get out of my depth. We all remember Lumbini.

I am bringing a little cash, no credit cards and no passport. When I am asked to transfer to a second bus I wonder if I've been too cavalier about this river trip. I don't have a change of clothes for one thing. Also I am wearing all cotton clothing. It doesn't dry fast and it keeps you colder for a longer period.

The guy next to me wants to switch seats. Then he wants a place in my foot well. Then he needs to stop the bus to buy a bag of potatoes from the side of the road. We are moving into cooler country and I now wonder how cold the water will be. I have had hypothermia once. It wasn't fun.

Running water splashes off cement basins in the ground. Big beautiful butterflies waft by on the wind. We're in the foothills now, mountain territory and terraced slopes. Whenever I reply that I am staying in Chitwan everyone reminds me how fucking hot it is in Chitwan.

At some point the conductor asks if I'm the rafting passenger.

He escorts me off the bus and we drift through a small patch of buildings on the side of the road with him peeking in each door looking for the guy I'm supposed to meet. This time the guy is where they said he would be. Responsibility for me is transferred from one man to the other and I am led to a bench outside the rafting hut. A group comprised of one middle aged big-bellied man wearing a "Love Don't Pay the Bills" t-shirt and six girls are suiting up.

"Where are you from?" he asks, fumbling with his life jacket.

"America." Which still sounds weird to me because I'm from Los Angeles.

"Good country," he says and then laughs when I say, "except we have a stupid president." They are from Delhi and I am not part of their group. Mine is en route from Kathmandu. A fuzzy white dog that looks exactly like Jenny barks at us from underneath the display case.

One of the guides walks through, "Bathroom far back on the left," he says to the crowd without stopping.

My fears about my state of preparedness are alleviated. For one thing I remember that I have packed a poncho and two I discover a shirt. YEAH!!! Also every one of the girls is wearing cotton pants, shirts and flip-flops. Three of the girls are wearing jewelry and don't look to be outdoorsy types. It's a three and a half hour boat trip that includes a stop for lunch. Then we will be delivered to a town where we will wait for the road to open up again at 4 p.m. Again someone promises me that they will get me loaded onto the right bus for my return to Chitwan.

The man and the girls take pictures of themselves with holding paddles. They wish me well and then one by one each grabs a paddle and follows their guide (he of the requisite gorgeous build) and they vanish down the slope on the other side of the road.

The dog crouching under the merchandise case only barks me now. Sean scored yesterday. A job interview. So he is ebullient now and calming my money fears and my guilt at having such a good time here which is due in no small part to Sandy. We want to do things and don't mind self-promoting ourselves so we are getting a great vacation. With our diverse interests we can't run out of things to do here. She made the elephant thing happen. I got her into the jungle. We are enjoying the town and the people. There is no one we won't talk to so there is no end to company if we want it.

Where the hell is my group? An enormous chicken and three chicks wander by.

A group exuding machismo steps off the bus. Twelve twenty-somethings from Kathmandu. The men preen and the girls giggle. They swagger in, run the chickens off and immediately take pictures of themselves wielding paddles. They haven't brought water because they are drinking beer to pass the time. They join me at the table and not one of them addresses me. Apparently we are waiting for two more, a couple from Canada. Roadblocks are holding them up.

The rafting trip comes and goes. It's a class three ride. We could bob babies in the current and they'd be safe. I'm glad for the trip and the river offers a nice break from the heat in Chitwan. Later on I will realize that I forgot sunblock. The river is overused. Pretty, but piles of trash hover at the water's edge and we fish out several empty water bottles out as we drift by.

While we wait in town for the busses that will take us home, the group fractures into its original components. We are informed that we can change clothes in the restaurant next to people eating lunch.

Apparently the highways that lead home are still blocked. Busses and cars line up in the street waiting for the signal that the roads are clear. Our guide takes me from bus to bus until he finds a driver who agrees to take me on. It's a three-hour drive back to the taxi stand.

Ten minutes after traffic starts up I realize that I am ill and that I will be lucky to get to the taxi stand before I need a bathroom. I pant for the next three hours to keep from shitting in my seat.

The guy behind me is coughing and spitting so much that the man sitting next to him moves to the back of the bus to sit on the floor rather than continue to endure his disgusting companion's behavior.

I pant and hold on. I am so close to shitting in my seat. I make it without being disgusting but after I stumble off the bus and find a taxi-man I have to run to the bathroom and then have to lie on the ground before I can climb into the man's cab. It's a 30-minute cab drive. I try to pay the driver but I have to get to my knees for a minute to keep from being sick.

"Are you alright Madam?" he says when I get back to my feet. I make it to the bathroom in time. Whatever they fed us at lunch has made me ill.

Key Differences: A forest is defined as a large area that is covered with trees and underbrush. It is also referred to as wood or woods. ... A forest is marked by a large covered area with tall trees, whereas a jungle is marked by a concentrated area with dense shrubs, grasses and shorter trees (Wikipedia, 2018).

SECOND JEEP TREK

I have convinced Sandy and the new girl, a Chinese woman who is a badass bargain hunter to come along on this last jeep journey.

I seem to remember something about Chinese culture and money when I see the Chinese woman bargain, but maybe I'm just racist. Mindful of my experience on my last jeep trip, I told her and Sandy about the rainstorm, so she wants to buy a rain jacket. She gets it for half the price I paid.

"Madame, you are my first customer today, so I am giving you a discount already. 800."

"500," She says softly.

"Madame I am not cheating you this a fair price."

"500," as if she has 800, but he's not getting it.

"800. It is a good jacket." He smiles at her politely

"Yes, for 500." She smiles politely back.

"700 Madame." I am horrified at the whole process because I am not a bargainer. I walk to the front of the store with Sandy and we peruse postcards of tigers and rhinoceroses fucking.

"500 I think."

"That is very cheap. 600."

"500 is better. That is what I will pay."

"500 Madame." In instantly think of the seven things I bought this week for what now seems like twice the price.

We have time and Sandy and I wanted to introduce the new girl to our favorite restaurant before the trek, but a relative of one of the owners has died and so the business is closed for the rest of the day which is when Sandy clarifies the fact that today rather than tomorrow is my last day and just like that I'm done here. So we eat down by the river so we can watch for animals while we eat. The new girl orders a local dish, which turns out to be dried flattened rice that she cannot chew.

No hint of rain in the sky today.

It's a good group in this Jeep. An Indian couple with a baby, an excitable German woman, Sandy, me, and the new girl. For whatever reason I seem to be seeing animals more than the others. So people start tapping me on the shoulder and requesting a view of specific animals as if

I have the magic touch.

We only see pieces of a sloth bear (see patch of fur in the picture on the left below) because the beast moves so quickly through the foliage that we only see him in the spaces between bushes, grass and trees. I see a flash of black, a piece of a brown nose, more black body and a black ass and he's gone too quickly for anyone to have taken a picture, but man, were we all excited to have seen him. The mom is working hard to keep the baby from crying all the while.

We stop to watch a humungous female rhino that decides that we are worthy of a closer look. She is magnificent and not afraid of us. She crosses the meadow, stops when she reaches the road, and seems to consider running us down. The Jeep driver shifts into reverse in anticipation of a charge, but she changes her mind and just crosses to the other side but not before turning and giving us the best view of something else gorgeous that is the last of her kind. I don't have a notebook so I am writing notes on my sunburnt legs.

Closer to the crocodile breeding center a wild boar and her four striped babies race across the road in front of us ducking into the bush where she vanishes, but the babies stop and give us time for some snapshots. A jeep filled with blind tourists coming the other way forces us to edge off the road. I don't know. You figure that one out.

Peacocks and Peahens race along the road next to us. Stripped deer standing too deeply in the jungle to photograph stare us down. The crunch of tires on crushed gravel signals the turn into the breeding center and the sow with her babies zip across the road again.

No water and no food left to buy once we get to the crocodile center. It's late in the day. All supplies have been bought by other tourists. I'm melting but I still visit the crocodile pools to stare at animals whose habitat we have destroyed.

We don't see much on the way back but cross paths with several other jeeps in which we see tourists we now know. Five minutes of conversation before you board your boat is all it takes to know that person in the swirl of strangers that becomes a constant in our lives. Someone needs something and strangers reply because we are together and alone on our journeys. I love traveling.

JUNE 1, LAST DAY IN CHITWAN

Because of the heat life happens in the mornings and at night in Chitwan. Daytime proper is for napping. Shops are unattended in the middle of the day while the owners lie on the floor in the coolest place they can find. I love the informality of that. If you come in the middle of the day you yell "Namaste!" until someone yells it back which means, "I'm coming." Also someone else noticing that you are in the shop will RUN to get the clerk who might then emerge from the field herding ducks or leading a goat that she/he has to secure before she/he can help you.

It's pre-storm so goddamn it is hot and the traveler's sickness yesterday made me very ill for precisely four hours, so that's a good thing, but I still feel fragile. I went from lying on the ground in the middle of the village with people asking "Madam, are you alright?" to now when I'm just purged and a little weak. I can only keep down Orange Fanta and coconut cookies, but I am recovered. I have another jungle trek schedules for this afternoon that I don't want to miss so I'm just writing and picture taking today. I'm also preparing to test my digestive tract at the local coffee shop. The sign says open at 9. In Nepali time this means, likely this morning, sometime before noon.

I'll wait.

Chitwan is a bicycle town. Parents sit their kids on the back of their bikes or balance them in their laps. There's also a fair amount of motorcycle traffic. Visitors do not need licenses or helmets. On motorbikes you see two or even three kids stuffed in between their parents as they putt, putt away. In Cambodia I saw as many as six people on one bike. All your genetic hopes and dreams in one basket. Although the general rule is, "keep to the left," I don't know why there aren't constant accidents, everyone and everything uses the whole road.

I just realized that today is my last day here.

The kids are headed to school now. Green and grey, and blue and black uniforms with hair braided and tied back or carefully combed back. These newly minted people race along the streets chittering and gabbing. If they see you they wave, "HELLO!" Or they clasp their hands together and yell "Namaste!" as one. (Essentially, hello, bye, hi, have a good day and, I bow to the light within you all in one.) The mothers with smaller children and babies sit on raised platforms because it's a place that regularly floods and wave. Even the babies know to clasp their hands together, when you pass by, "Namaste!" No one smiles as broadly as these kids do. I may fold and buy the football Ayush asked me for as well as some toys for the other kids at the stable, and some mangoes for the elephants and I have some family shots of the people who run the inn that I think I will develop at home and mail back.

It's about time to travel into the mountains for the trekking portion of my trip. I can't believe that I feel so at home in a place that I've been in for such a short time. I felt this way about the southern African countries too. The sad thing about these places is the urbanization. Trash heaps, hotels, tour agencies, a pace of life being altered to fit the world outside and the death of the wilderness that drew outsiders here in the first place. These places or cultures aren't perfect, but wilderness should be defended for its own sake, tooth and nail, now especially. And all these cultures have some horrible aspects that need to be exorcised, but you can do that without stripping them of their uniqueness.

I'm sure I'd get tired of this place too after a while. There is a level of animal cruelty that is hard to accept. I want to spend a day picking up trash and ordering people to do the same. There is no doubt that I am a city girl, but for just now these places allow you to hear yourself, to be close to other people in ways that get annihilated at home.

POKHARA AND ANNAPURNA

I like it when there's a guy standing next to plane you are boarding, nodding at the passengers and leaning against a fire extinguisher the size of an eight year old. I like it when I look out the window of a plane that holds 18 people and see a dent in the wing that's been hammered out. No seat for the attendant. I don't know what she does. I am however accompanied by a 17 year old whose mother saw me sitting alone in the Bharatpur airport and instructed her daughter to join me. The girl is very sweet.

I was already watching her earlier. They don't speak English in this airport so I needed to find someone taking my flight—in order to stalk them, you know, like a serial killer does. Nothing suspicious about the white woman sitting behind you, that's how I read your ticket.

It's a two and half hour wait because, Nepali time, then we climb into the small tube with wings. I duck because the ceiling is too low and find my seat. The attendant walks up the aisle with a basket of weird tasting candies and that gets handed back until someone empties it.

20 minutes later, a brutal landing. I also love it when the plane hops—three times. (I only scream on the inside) and we are in Pokhara, a more traditional tourist city.

At our first meeting my guide informs me that although the first day of the trek will "be nothing." The second and third days will be hours of straight uphill.

"Like Namche?" I say. The trek from the bottom of the hill in the Himalayas up into the Namche Bazaar is a way to destroy all that is soft inside you.

"Yes," he nods cheerfully.

"But, no leeches, right." It's a thing with me now.

He shrugs. "If no rain, no."

Alright Kim, man the fuck up. This WILL BE FUN. "8:30 tomorrow?"

"Yes, of course," he says.

Tonight I will order a massive heart stopper meal from the hotel.

(And hey, when I was really ill, a doctor's visit, antibiotics, probiotics, and electrolyte solution cost $6.81 USD)

ANNAPURNA

One night in a luxurious hotel in Pokhara has left me feeling toasted. I paid for a body scrub and a massage. Living simply is exhausting. And living out of your backpack is freeing and tiring. You never leave anything behind when you step out the door, but then you also need to be constantly vigilant.

"Where's my stuff?"

"Is anyone going to take my stuff?"

"Are you looking at my stuff?"

I like wandering. I like being responsible for my own water supply, my own food and measuring out how much time there's left in the battery because there is no more electricity today, etc. I also like running on little or no food. It feels clean. Sean says (FACEBOOK POSTING chats) that I've lost weight. But one night in a bed, in an air-conditioned room reminds my body that it's stressed. There's an iconic National Geographic photograph of a stunning Afghani girl with bright green eyes someone took maybe twenty years ago. The face of the same girl 17 years later is burnt and her expression hardened by simple living. Point is that I'm tired. Once I start trekking I will revive. The idea of how hard the hike will be is worse than it will be.

I want to keep thinking about today and no further. I hope my shoes are up to the task ahead. It's only a six day hike. I didn't have a lot of time this trip, but I wanted to hike a little before I left. It's warm and sunny this morning, and colder than it is in Chitwan. It takes me several minutes to figure out the shower buttons. The body scrub I paid for yesterday inflamed my bug bites, but what you gonna do?

Philodendrons are in abundance, in the yard, in the lobby, by the pool, along the walls. The hotel is across the street from Phewa Lake, a major attraction in Pokhara, but my room overlooks the courtyard instead of the lake, and tall trees block the view of the lake from the street.

Yesterday the guide apologized for not picking me up at the airport. Then he apologized because the taxi driver who did pick me up first took me to the wrong hotel before bringing me here. "Sorry. Sorry. Sorry," he kept saying. I think it's the easy way to apologize if you don't know English very well. I do the same because I don't know any Nepalese. Sorry. Sorry. Sorry. This guide is very spare, confident and amenable to start. I wonder about Dunbar, the guide who took us to the Everest Base camp years ago. Is he still in Nepal? I remember that he wanted to emigrate and that he was looking for international connections. He didn't want to end up guiding all his life and he didn't want to end up in Dubai on some super dangerous construction site like his brother.

A dog barked outside the hotel last night. I got out of bed several times and looked out my window trying to locate the source of the sound. What did it need? How could I have helped? How could I go to sleep as long as it barked? Was it being ignored or unheard? I think about this shit at home too. At the edge of my imagination—all the ways animals can be hurt, as if it is my job to answer every cry.

This country is so beautiful but wherever people have touched it, they've trashed it, and as is true everywhere else, the importance of every wild thing is assessed in terms of its importance to people. Since most of you believe in God, when did God say that the garden exists for your sake?

Fuckers.

I am also nurturing hatred for a particular kind of tourist. I think of them as the devourers. They consume. They take pictures, but they don't see. They visit the villages, but they don't meet the villagers although they are often quite knowledgeable about the locals and their customs. Then there are the trekkers like me. Single women—age doesn't matter. When they are in my space I feel super aggressive at first and then we talk and I'm good. We are all alone in a good way with what we want to do and we are almost totally free of anyone else's expectations.

My husband is on a roll by the way. Loving him when I speak to him. I like living with him and I miss him, but maybe we need separate vacations, here and there.

I'm writing and taking breakfast downstairs while I wait for the guide and the driver. The hotel staff is dressed in khaki shirts and the fezzes. This disturbs me. I feel the need to salute my waiter. Drinking milk and eating fruit. Hoping that none of it backfires on me. I am also hoping that the medications I am taking, as prescribed in Chitwan, are good for me. I haven't been sick since I started dosing. A light dose of food poisoning and proactive care?

Feeling weepy and sentimental. Travel lets me come to the surface emotionally. I stop cramming who I am seven layers deep in order to complete my assigned tasks. All the home bullshit is gone and instantly I am a reader and a writer again. I am also a tea drinker here ... go figure.

I still have my eye open for gifts and I need to ask the Sherpa about tips. I can't tip everybody. I just can't. It's not only the only the cost, it's the expectation.

GUIDING

60% of the medical services administered on Everest are for the Sherpa. I am told that the services are subsidized. I guess this is the case because Everest is such a massive tourist attraction and Sherpa are generally paid for shit for their services. Many porters suffer from altitude illness. They are often pressed to go high and fast, carrying big loads and are reluctant to admit that they are sick because it might mean that they lose their jobs. So when they finally get help they have usually been sick for a few days and are in a worse state than the trekkers. A newspaper article I read described the Everest Basecamp as a warren of tents, trash and human excrement, which leads us back to my point about people thinking nature is to be used but not tended. Who the hell told you that you could shit on Everest and leave it there?

The days change now. They start early and end around 3 p.m. or so, sometimes earlier as the hikes are broken up into doable lengths and geography determines that. We don't stop for the rainstorms; there's no point in that although we do pass people huddled under shelters.

I feel bad. My guide seems uncomfortable with the fact that I am carrying my backpack. We agreed at the start that I would carry it until I tired but this arrangement didn't last long because he couldn't stand it. So now I try to keep his pace and when he starts to breathe heavier, I feel lazy and when he suggests we stop. We stop. Clouds in the sky, but they aren't the threatening kind. The guide says that there are a mixture of tribes living here and that they intermingle because community matters most. He lives in Kathmandu but comes from a village. He and his wife have one daughter and that is all they want because he says that he does not need a son.

When we arrive at our lunch stop the guide vanishes into the kitchen with the cook. I think this also gives him a break from me. I have many questions. I can't help it. He's seen a bear, but only in the village and he saw a tiger once. The bears descend seasonally and sometimes the cats come down to eat a cow or a goat. I dose with aspirin, caffeine, and sugared tea just in case a migraine is lurking about now that I am a little worn. When it comes to lunch all I want are liquids, tomato soup and sugared tea. I have a bag of these weird nuts I bought off a vendor in case I need more sustenance. A dog latched onto us a mile back. He comes and goes but always seems to catch up. He now rests by my side on a folded carpet piled with pillows. Someone sleeps outside here. The guide is on his iPhone. It is how we do privacy now. Everyone sits together and scrolls through their messages. Silverware is for tourists. Locals eat with their right hands mixing food with rice before they eat it. It's okay for the cats to jump onto the tables, which they do to get their share of food.

Trekking is a narrowing down process. The rooms you stay at get smaller the higher up you go. The teahouses (inns) are sometimes isolated so if you need particular items, buy them in town before you start your hike. We trek into a place to small to be called a village and the guide vanishes while I wait. This place is really four buildings stuffed into a corner of a mountain in between where we were this morning and where we want to go eventually. We are high up but we are also in a valley with houses nestled hundreds of feet overhead on severely slanted, tilled green slopes.

This turns out to be our final stopping off place for today. Chandra Guesthouse in a place too small to have a name. A dozen teens chattering in Nepali sit outside and share sodas and two men share a glass of water while they stretch out on carpet swatches. I can have a shower if I want to pay but I'd rather stew in my sweat until we return to civilization, not that we are very far away. A four-hour hike after a two-hour drive from Pokhara. I can hear but not see the river. The constant trilling of crickets underscores all the other sounds, even more than the birdcalls. Rainclouds have moved in cutting off the mountaintops.

The guide leads me to my room, opens the door with a huge brass key, enters the room and swings my pack onto my bed. Then he hands me the key and vanishes. I could get phone service, if I had a phone but no Internet. Hundreds of beer bottles are stacked up against the building below me. An effort to keep the place clean. I can't imagine drinking and trekking. And

I can't figure out how the people living in the hills overhead get supplies on a regular basis. This is lower Himalaya territory so the breathing is much easier. I've had no problems so far.

They grow corn, beans, spinach, cabbage, peaches, and oranges in these hills and trade or sell what they don't use in Pokhara. The guide insists that he is not Buddhist. I'm don't ask what he is. Don't care. It won't matter if it rains today but I wish it would wait for five more days. The guide makes much of the fact he knew Dumbar who guided Sean and me years ago because usually trekkers request the same staff and he wants me to know they tried to get him.

One foot in front of the other as we hike. I can see my meditation practice coming into play. I have always hiked this way. I keep my eyes off the goal. I pay attention to where I am, but meditation has sharpened my awareness of keeping to center. Five prayer flag colors. The guide says that blue represents the heavens, red represents fire and the sun, while white represents wind, green for water and yellow for earth. He also says that Hindus code the flags another way and tries to explain these to me but all I know for sure is that the flags can also be used in times of crisis and conflict and mean different things during these times.

Aside from Namaste I don't know what people are saying to the guide as we pass by them on the road but there's always some conversation. I feel as if we are walking through his hometown and all the Nepali gang is here, everywhere we go. I feel dizzy not as in vertigo or illness, but something is buzzing inside me and I feel like I can't focus but here I am writing so that's not the case. I miss the safety of Sean's company. He keeps me from turning too much into myself. There's only so much me I need to know about me at any one time.

Roosters seem to crow all day long here. At least there aren't any dogs barking. My heart needs a rest. How the hell did they get phone lines up here and come to that, I am stunned by how much work it must have taken to build all these steps that make up most of the road we are traveling over (the last ¼ mile or so) today. Who terraced the ground? Who cut the steps (by hand) out of the rock and who hauled these thick slate slabs all up here and layered the ground with them?

There are steps up and down leading from one settlement to the next and lanes leading through the shops and teahouses in the bigger tourist stops. The teahouses look like old style train stations to me but much smaller. Six tables sometimes as much as eight set inside buildings with windows all around. The windows are all open now. Window frames are set six inches above the tables so that anyone sitting down is on display to those passing by. All the teahouses boast *"24 hours hot water and electricity."* A bold statement that. Someone is playing a flute in the valley below. Not loudly enough that I can recognize a tune but it's a constant sound.

JUNE 3, MY GRANDFATHER'S BIRTHDAY— THE NEXT GUESTHOUSE

All the buildings, all the machinery, all the boards, nails, hasps, roof tops and door frames and handles, all the floor boards are rickety, rusty and crudely hewn. Solidly assembled without a ruler or an eye toward a refined finish. The buildings stand out, brightly colored but not an eye pleaser. Likely someone brought all the raw materials necessary for construction up the mountain on their backs. Not even a dray beast could or would cart this shit up here. I don't see any anyway. A few goats, some buffalo, chickens, cats and dogs. So no hauling houses uphill, except at the expense of human labor. There's a bird black with a white ring about its neck running underneath the tables in the dining room. I first heard it scuffling under the tables and then saw its black feet moving very quickly through the room. Ah, up on a table, out the open window and into the forest. What's the difference between a forest and a jungle? I may need my cold stuff tonight. There's a massive bamboo growth in front of me just outside this window, three stories high. Holy hell it's huge.

I'm told Ghorepani is next. There's really no need to give me names of places. I won't remember them.

A mosquito is buzzing around.

Not wanting to spend any more time in the cramped space of my bedroom than I have to, I sit in the open dining area where I can read and write under the protection of the semi-enclosed space; but also so that I can be outside and hear the ducks call and the low level buzzing of the crickets roll against the sound of the river, a milky glacial melt, as it heads past the power plant and into Pokhara eventually filling Phewa Lake. The smell of wet wood mixed with incense, someone is praying, dissipates by the time it hits the teahouse. When it gets to me there's just a hint of smoke in the air. I'm exhausted but I don't want to go to sleep too early.

A black-faced macaw reveals herself just outside my window. She stops to stare at me but not for long. I'm not food, another monkey or a predator. She has no use for me. If I watch all the trees I can see several more monkeys racing along the branches. One thick one in particular is being used as a preferred passage between two big trees. The monkeys change the way the trees sway, I don't know if they can see me but they don't seem to care. It's like watching a fish tug on a line. They keep coming from one direction to the other. There must be a hidden part of the circle I can't see. Then I do see three large and several small figures that seem to settle in the crooks of one big tree. No, my mistake, they are still moving everywhere taking from the trees as they go. Suddenly I see bigger, heftier fleshed out figures vs. the smaller spidery types. Then the cook comes out and whistles and they all flee, vanishing so quickly that it's like watching fairies wink out of sight.

The cook hands me a massive plate of macaroni and cheese. I can't place the taste of the sauce or the cheese but it's enough. And he places a massive fruit plate next to the pasta. Apples, cinnamon and honey. Where are you Sean? I need you. It's not easy to go into these small rooms with two cots that Sean and I pushed together and fell asleep on when we traveled here last time. I don't look forward to that particular point of solitude even if it's only for three or four nights.

AS TOLD TO ME BY THE GUIDE

The entire massif and surrounding area are protected within the 7,629 square kilometres (2,946 sq mi) Annapurna Conservation Area, the first and largest conservation area in Nepal. Established in 1985.

Nepal is mostly Hindu (80%), Buddhists (15%) and others.

Upper *Mustang*, located in the trans-Himalayan region of western *Nepal*, a critical and endangered .... It has an area of 2,567 sq. kms. It is a restricted trekking area of Nepal located in the Northern part of Nepal. Mustang was only open for visitors after 1992. Before, visitors were not allowed to enter the forbidden kingdom of Mustang.

It includes a dry area isolated by two mountains called Mustang (2567km) unlike the rest of Nepal it is not green but a desert, and for some time it has been its own kingdom but part of Great Nepal which is the result of unification of some 16 kingdoms. The last king voluntarily gave up power in 2008 to allow Nepal to become a republic. Though still recognized by many Mustang residents, the monarchy ceased to exist on October 7, 2008, by order of the Government of Nepal. The last official and later unofficial king who traced his lineage directly back to Ame Pal, the warrior who founded this Buddhist kingdom in 1380.

Wikipedia says that King Gyanendra's seven-year reign began in tragedy. According to their information, Gyanendra inherited the throne after 10 members of the royal family were massacred by Crown Prince Dipendra in 2001 and floundered. It the end he was given 15 days to leave the palace which was turned into a museum.

An elected assembly drew up a new constitution that backed the creation of a republic in the Himalayan nation, which endured 10 years of war against Maoist rebels, who are now the dominant partners in the new political firmament.

If I understand the guide correctly though, he tells the story about a magnanimous ruler who abdicated because he loved his people and knew the time had come for Nepal to move into the modern age and become a republic. Since the communist were involved, I wonder if my guide isn't a communist. Just saying. Not that I believe anybody.

The influence of the outside world, especially China, is growing and contributing to rapid change in the lives of Mustang's people. Tourism to Upper Mustang is regulated. Foreigners need to obtain a special permit to enter, costing US$50 per day per person. Most tourists travel by foot over largely the same trade route used in the 15th century.

The southern third of the district is called Thak and is Thakali homeland of whose culture combines Tibetan and Nepalese elements. Very unique Buddhists. Life in Mustang revolves around tourism, animal husbandry and trade.

Mustang was once an independent kingdom, although closely tied by language and culture to Tibet. From the 15th century to the 17th century, its strategic location granted Mustang control over the trade between the Himalayas and India. At the end of the 18th century the kingdom was annexed by Nepal and became a dependency of the Kingdom of Nepal since 1795. Upper Mustang is won an ancient trade route between Nepal and Tibet exploiting the lowest 4,660 metres (15,300 ft.) pass Kora La through the Himalaya west of Sikkim. This route remained in use until China's annexation of Tibet in 1950.

Then my guide tells me about the Gurka soldiers of Nepalese descent many of whom lived in India and were recruited by the British. He said that they also served in what was known as the Gurkha Contingent in Singapore, the Gurkha Reserve Unit Brunei, the United Nations Peace Keeping force, and in war zones around the world. Historically, "Gurkha" and "Gorkhali" were synonymous with "Nepali." The name may be traced to medieval Hindu warrior-saint Guru Gorakhnath who has a historic shrine in Gorkha. The word means protector. The Gorkha tribes united the Gorkha Kingdom and fought against the British invasions. Gurkhas are associated with the Khukuri, a forward-curving Nepalese knife, and have always had a reputation for fearless military prowess. According to Wikipedia, former Indian Army Chief of Staff Field Marshal Sam Manekshaw, once stated that, "if a man says he is not afraid of dying, he is either lying or he is a Gurkha."

When the British Empire came to South Asia, Gorkha tribes who united the Gorkha Kingdom in the first place fought against the British invasions but eventually began serving the British in Army regiments traveling around the world soldiering.

There are:

- 125 difference ethnic groups in Nepal
- 100 different spoken languages
- Nepali is the national language.

Greater Nepal ("Undivided Nepal") was the result of the unification movement of all the kingdoms.

Gurung people also called Tamu, are an ethnic group from different parts of Nepal. Until the 15th century they were ruled by a Gurung king.

Terms I learned but forgot how they fit into the stories my guide was telling me because he talked faster than I could take notes:

- Kola Shothar (3rd home) Gurung ancient home
- Ajimo bajimgo-demon
- Guru Ringobche (Padmasambhava ("Lotus-Born"),/ 8th-century Indian Buddhist master. he is venerated as a "2nd Buddha" by adherents of in Tibet, Nepal, Bhutan, the Himalayan states of India, and elsewhere

- 4 sons (4 caste system Gurung)
- 11 casts Gurung
- Kershing Gunung (mtn. in Nepal?)
- Phile phiandre
- Devi (Sanskrit word for "goddess")

This is the end of my history lesson for this night.

After my guide gives me his speech he disappears again.

NEXT NIGHT'S LESSON

MYTH: Kola Shothar (3rd home)

A demon called Ajimo Bajingo killed three kings. Each time this happened the people moved, finally arriving at Kola Shothar, their third home. At this point a large group of children wander off and find a very ugly man but he is unique and clearly an entity of some power. They return home and bring their people to him. When he wakes, they ask him if he can kill the demon that is hunting their tribe. He says that he will for 1 massive bag of flour, 1 goat and 1 massive bag of cider. They comply. The battle rages for three days and three nights. When the demon is finally killed this creature, Guru Ringboche or Padme Shamba, says that he must now leave because he is needed in many places. The people beg him to stay. He finally agrees if someone will offer their daughter to marry him. No one wants to because he is so ugly. So all the girls who present themselves to him they try to look as ugly as possible.

He selects and marries Sara, their tribe is Buddhist but unique Buddhists (I am not certain if they are Theravadan or not and sources do not agree). They have four sons which results in four castes. Another pair Devi and Phile Philandre have 16 sons (16 castes). Both groups practice brother/sister marriage. There is a test. They set two fires, and if the smoke from both mingle then the marriages should proceed. If the smoke doesn't mix the marriages will be bad and are stopped.

Gurung people predominate in this region. Today in the isolate mountain regions are tribes that still practice castes system and inter-marriage but it is not okay in modern culture-education, as mixing with other cultures and a modern sense of morality forbids it.

MY DREAM

We are on a small lake. I am part of a small group of students, all Hispanic, some from Peru. Who the hell knows why my dream got that specific? We all like each other. I know no one's name. All the girls have long thick curly black hair. All the men have black thick hair. Everyone was dark skinned except for two fair people, me and another fat girl. Our school's name is something hokey.

We break into pairs to complete our tasks, the first of which was to sail across this very small lake. I have a bird's eye view of this lake. The lake is round and surround by greenery. The sailboats have a narrow tongue up front like the canoes in Chitwan. It can dip into the water without threatening to sink the boat. One partner sails the boat while the other collects items needed in order to complete other tasks. There are no sharks in the water, which for me never happens. In all my dreams water = sharks, but this water is completely safe. I have so much fun sailing. My partner is so good at maneuvering the boat that I forget to collect any items the first time we circle the lake.

Then we arrive at the school buildings on the other side.

We are told to select a painting from five or six in a catalogue and to call the place from this sailing school saying we were from the school and ask them to paint the painting we had selected. The paintings were all of animals cartoon style and very pretty but not realistic.

We were in line for the phone in a room that was painted a gentle color and completely bare except for the telephone and a girl hanging midair against the opposite wall. I have a sense of a TV being on in the background but don't ever see or hear it and a sense of being watched but benignly and passively. The phone is only a receiver attached to the wall by a chord, all of which vanishes after we use it.

After one of the students before us calls he hands the receiver over to us and sees the girl and goes over to her and they hug one another as if they had known one another for a long time. I notice their feet.

But by the time it is our turn to call there is only blank canvass left to paint on. My partner and I are offered two square inches of it and are informed that next time there will be more paintings to choose from.

NEXT MORNING:
THE SECOND DAY OF OUR HIKE

A dog, a biscuit colored fuzzy-wuzzy thing, is curled up on the steps beneath my room. When I walk down to wash my face in the outdoor sink it wags its tail furiously as I approach hoping that I won't make it move. I step around it and wish it good morning. I do the same thing when I return to my room. While inside I hear someone else pass the dog and grouch at it. Looking out the door see a trekker wave the dog off the steps. The dogs here don't seem to fight. They are territorial, but I've yet to see bloodshed.

Really slept well last night. Goddamn, I reached a deep dreaming state. Everyone who stayed here last night is up early. There are long hikes ahead for all. We are all groggy. I am the only woman here. I need to buy water. Coffee is beautiful. This teahouse is an aerie. It's the kind of tree house you hoped to have built when you were a kid. I still can't figure how the people living in the side of the steep mountains live there or how they build those nice houses into the rock like that.

Happy Birthday Grandfather. I am thinking of you and my bitch mother today. You have all these relationships with people you will never see again on these trips and starting new relationships reminds me of longstanding ones. I used to think it was okay to litter on school property and in movie theatres, but WTF. A trail of ants are using a branch that connects two trees twenty feet apart 100 feet off the ground like a highway. There are two discernable lanes of traffic. Talk about safe passage. Who is going to step on them there? Does my guide who serves me make my meals too?

You are in *it* here. You can't change the weather. You can't manage the heat or the cold. You can't step out of the rain. You can't remove the bugs from the equation. You can only become a willing part of the system affected by *what is* instead of changing the environment to suit your taste so you step into *it* and become part of the system, as malleable as it is, as out of control of it as any other animal or element and in so doing you see what you are more clearly than if you could step inside or flip a switch and change the situation or even change how you feel about it. The environment controls all that. I think everyone who lives here learns that which is why to the western eye these people look passive. They aren't. They are integral parts of the system and are active in that sense but a westerner who sees himself as a terra-former (in order to be successful in his mind) can't make sense of that point of view. He thinks he would be erased if he became integral as the others are. He needs to make a contradictory stand or he feels as if he doesn't matter and so destruction is his sound of self. Destruction becomes his way of being known.

TIME TO GO TO GHOREPANI

For lunch at Mountain View Guest House & Restaurant: a milk shake with banana, sweetened ginger tea and potato soup.

European bathrooms means that you don't have to squat over a hole and that toilet paper will be available instead of just a hose although the paper cannot go into the toilet and must be packed out.

"Please," also means—*PAY ATTENTION*

Buddhist Prayer Flags: Blue   White   Red   Green   Yellow

Buddhist Prayer: Om   mani   Padme   hum

A cloud canopy has moved in blocking off the sun but it's not dark and I don't hear thunder. Hopefully it's just a traveling cluster of wet. I have a plastic bag to protect my camera and my new raincoat in my pack just in case things turn nasty. My iPhone and Kindle are in ziplock bags. A television is on somewhere. I can't understand the language, but the program sounds very soapy. Although I bought some dried fruits and nuts from a stall at the base of the hike to supplement my diet, my appetite goes away the higher we get so I put the nuts away and eat for warmth and to hydrate instead.

There are Massive Roosters here. I bet one of them could take on one of my girls (dogs). Seriously, when they crow it's a sonorous booming sound.

Pro Tip: Bathroom lights are placed on the outside of outhouses here. I realize this every time I step inside and shut the door. Total blackness when you know that there's a gross hole nearby is bad.

The teahouses are colorful and all decked out with souvenirs. I'll wait until Pokhara. I really don't want to carry more things with me up the hill than I have to.

A 6 hour trek today. Although we rest often, I spend most of the day dogging my guide's steps because he's carrying the pack. We walk a slow and steady pace for a long time. The trail winds up over something like 3,500 steps placed in between stretches of raw trail and several suspension bridges. We play leapfrog with other trekkers all day long.

My guide tells me about Gorka soldiers and compulsory Nepalese enlistment in the Falkland wars, among other English endeavors. If I understand him, Gorka/Nepalese forces, including civilians of all ages and genders, fought the British at one point making the kind of blood sacrifice that finally convinced the Brits to back off. He disputes the story that I was told the last time I was in Nepal, about the royal prince murdering his family and shooting himself in the head. He says it is fodder for conspiracy theorists and that actually someone else assassinated the popular prince and his family. I tell him about the Kennedy assassination and we talk about the mistake called Trump and about how Nepalese were holding their breaths wanting Clinton to win. Sandy said the same thing.

As we hike we pass chickens, horses (ponies that can carry your bags), buffalo standing in front of a bridge, dogs, kids, women squatting on the ground plucking vegetables, weeding, and washing clothes by slamming them against rocks and finally an old lady feeding a cat on the table from her plate.

A single trekker shares a chocolate bar with me. He says that he's damned tired of the steps and wants to know when the flat part begins. He is in a good mood. Although he has plans he says he will see how he feels as time goes on in terms of how far he will actually hike. I tell him about Sean and my Everest trip and admit that I didn't get to the basecamp because I became ill. We pass trekkers with walking sticks. They still seem like extra stuff to me. Are we in a Rhododendron forest? Is the Nepal national flower red?

I ask my guide (yes, he told me his name, but I can't remember it. Bad tourist!) about the symbols on the Nepalese flag and I'm not satisfied with his answer. He says something about revolution, which leads to talk about Eddie Izzard's monologue about flags. Now I hear a goat bleating and I need to know where that sound is coming from. The rain hits when we are about 40 minutes from our next stop. But we just put on our raingear and keep going. I walk more carefully because my running shoes are not made for slick rock and because my little leech friends are coming to life in the wet mud.

When we register at the police station, just before we get to the teahouse I will sleep in tonight, we decide to wait for the rain to ease up before we move on. I watch leeches inch worm across the slate tiles and hear the bells of a train of horses moving up the trail as their driver urges them on. The rain gets worse then suddenly the guide just seems to know. "We go," he says. Up we go and the rain lets up the instant we leave our shelter. We climb the last sodden steps to the teahouse in bright sunlight.

There will be no electricity for a few hours yet. An old style furnace in the middle of the dining room lets me know it will be cold tonight. I have a private bath but if I want a hot shower I have to drop money into a box first. There is all kinds of bullshit in my socks, I don't know how. My feet are bleeding from punctures but I only pull one leech out of my socks. Half the sky is clear and sunny and the other is still shrouded. The sunny part is as warm as the cloudy part is cold—go figure.

I've burned through two pens this trip. We start out at 4 a.m. tomorrow to hike to the viewpoint for Annapurna so that we can see it in sunrise. I worry about the rain. I'll dress for the cold I guess and bring a hefty bag.

ANOTHER DREAM

There isn't any magic to interpreting this one. I'm at a job. My boss is out. She's left me several autopsy files to evaluate. I am sitting at a messy desk outside with a knitted maroon afghan. My old friend Elisabeth, who is no longer my friend in real life, sits at the desk across from me. My work is projected onto a big screen so she can see it. I can't make sense of the pages and she complains about my lack of comprehension and says that she doesn't know why I still have my job. I struggle to understand what I am supposed to do all day and get nowhere. Elisabeth goes home at the end of the day and I decide to take work home with me so that I don't have to come in Saturday.

My boss (a new one) is there when I return. She is friendly, but is too busy to talk to me. She notices my messy desk and says my stepfather told her about my disorder and I say it's funny that I'm such a good writer because writing is about organization and I am messy. Then she drives off in a golf cart. She has people to talk to. I leave with my files. I'll just return with the work done Monday. Meanwhile I take a jacket that belongs to my brother (or father) and throw it away but not before I take a ten-dollar bill I've found in a pocket and stuff it into my pants pocket. Then I drive away into a dark L.A. landscape dark that is populated with 1000s of lighted homes and no streets, like in San Fernando hills used to be.

I was reading a book about a Quebec coroner who is worried about keeping her job when I fell asleep. My boss Claudia was on the phone talking about being from L.A. with some stranger. I am on an outdoorsy vacation. I made an afghan blanket once. The jacket and the money—that's the past. David, my stepfather often says surprising and stupid things about me to other people. Elisabeth is very judgy, which is why we aren't friends anymore. And I used to live in the San Fernando Valley. Fuck if I know what the golf carts are all about.

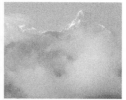

I am up at 10:30 and midnight and 12:30 and 2:30 and 3:41 after having anxiety dreams about stuff I can do nothing about while I am here. I get dressed in the dark and join the line of trekkers intent on reaching Poon—the viewpoint to see Annapurna at sunrise. It's a 45-minute hike up hundreds of steps. Gotta love steps. It starts to rain which amps my anxiety about *my stuff.* It doesn't take long before we are all stripped down to our tank tops and blue jeans. We are fine as long as we keep moving. It's only when we stand still that we get cold.

My guide and I pass four girls searching their socks for leeches, a woman who worries because I don't remember her from yesterday, a Cambodian who is here by way of Melbourne and a European businessman who is talking to his guide disrespectfully. "What are you doing?!" he says as he rips his iPad from his guide's hands.

We get up top to share and enjoy—clouds. She's (the mountain we can't see) there somewhere, so they say. It's a great view anyway. I take a grim picture of me in front of a sign. Then while waiting for the sun, I climb the viewing tower where I enjoy banter with other trekkers from all over the world. Then I pay a guy who is selling hot liquids. Hot water 100 - rupees. *Really guy?* I take a few pictures. One guy sets up a camera on a tripod to take shots automatically and I realize that my iPhone takes better pictures than my camera.

We don't need any of the warm clothing we brought with us.

A Huge White Moth demands my attention before it flies off.

Even through the cloud cover the mountains present as cutting edges in the sky in the rising pale light that makes the clouds glow and brings the landscape to life.

It is worth the walk.

Annapurna never really shows her face, but the majesty of this place is undeniable. I'm done waiting for her to show before the others and I am the first to head back down to breakfast. We retreat down the steps in the gentle rain. I have six hours of trekking ahead of me today and I am anxious to see if I can avoid the afternoon showers that are bound to come today. No internet. No phone. No more charge in my Kindle.

My love of reading has been revived. THANK GOD. Teaching kills it. In three weeks I've read ten novels (at night and during bus and plane rides). I've forgotten how good reading is for the soul (if we had one). When I get back to the teahouse I take out my notebook and kill a moth by accident. A serving of cornbread is about ten inches across here and four inches thick. I can't dry my clothes because they only light a fire at night.

They call me "sister" here. "Excuse me Sister we don't have peanut butter here, is honey okay?"

As the sun rises the view gets worse because the mist moves in.

After breakfast we pack up and begin the trek back down towards Pokhara.

They are all measured steps. The ground is a living thing. It's muddy. It's wet. It is mobile, so I focus on every one of the 15,000 steps that I need to take before we reach our destination. When walking in the rain, I am walking down a waterfall with several kinds of parasites brushing by my legs. This step looks slick, but it's not. That one looks textured, but it's slick. That one moves. That's a tree root. That step bends dropping me into a sandy depression. Prudence demands that I step up slowly and step down carefully. When the rain comes I cover up and keep walking. Standing in the rain or hiding underneath a makeshift shelter only means our destination is further away. Step. Step. Step. Step. Let the guy just ahead of me, who just stumbled, get a few extra steps ahead. We pass a bend in the river where a hundred cairns are stacked. A small sheltered statue of Buddha, holding a stick of incense in its hands, rests underneath a granite outcrop around the next bend. Someone has strung a single strand of prayer flags across the trail here. Up the path a ways someone else has strung up dozens and twisted them around a massive tree trunk.

We play leapfrog with other travelers who started out in the same place we did this morning. Everyone stops at different places for lunch. Everyone rests at alternate stops. We don't know one another's names, but we learn faces and wave as we pass each other again and again until people pull out of the slow race at their final stops. And the walking is forever. Eventually you didn't start anywhere and you're going nowhere. You are just walking until the blue face of your teahouse pops into view. Go inside. Go upstairs (always upstairs). The guide drops your pack and you separate until dinner when he will take your order. It's hard not to feel colonial when you have a guide. They carry your pack. They take your meal orders and they serve you and they seem offended if you stop them from doing their jobs.

The bridges are magic and often colonized by beasts: buffalo, horses, and long-haired goats. We pass a herd of goats sheltering from the storm several feet away from their caretakers, weathered wizened types, who are heating soup inside their tents and barking at the individual goats that look as if they might stray.

"Oh, I never get tired of trekking," a young man says to me at the next stop where I don't feel like paying for a shower and I don't have a towel. Don't know where that went to, so I peel off my clothes, remove all leech stowaways and hit the bed for a bit and fall into another dream.

I am in a relationship with two men. I am living with three people, them and a friend. The relationships are dying and the men are being cavalier shits about this, but haven't yet moved out. I'm reacting by scratching, yelling and punching them, which is not causing them any pain or making them react. They are enjoying their lives. The screen to the back door is broken by one of the men, a blond guy an actor from some show I've watched but can't remember now. One of the boyfriends is a young fuzzy haired blond.

One of the friends in the car with me is the kid who used to run triathlons. We talk about the show he's on and about a girl who used to be popular, but isn't now. He's a composite character, as is another dream friend. They are young, late teens/early 20's. We are in a parking lot that's broken up so badly in one spot that there's a huge hump and unpaved portions that I try to navigate in a beat up rusty orange dodge that's coughing smoke.

I try to buy furniture in this store. I look up after pressing a button and on screen the furniture ensemble is put together for me with a receipt printing out from a machine at the end. When I go to collect my furniture, it's not up yet. This salesman looks over my shoulder while I wait because I shouldn't be at the machine unless I have a receipt being printed. I turn and yell at him as loud as possible "You are pissing me off!"

The girl who is not popular anymore and I talk to triathlon kid about the scene in which his character appears. I don't know the two other people in my car. Michael Boatman is the manager of the furniture store. He remarks how my behavior is affecting everyone in the store but doesn't do much about it. He's not upset. Oprah Winfrey is lying in a lush round pink frilly bed set. I tell her the furniture set it too expensive and she reminds me that she has a credit for that exact amount and since the furniture is for her benefit that's perfect, which is why I go talk to Boatman in the first pace. Then I try to find a guy to fix my screen door by looking in the old big black phonebook that I used to own. I look for the section with fix-it men. Remembering a particular guy I want to hire cause he wanted the work so badly, but I can't exactly remember who he is exactly. I am feeling unknown and undervalued throughout this whole dream.

FOR REAL, THERE ARE A FUCKING LOT OF FLYING BUGS IN MY BEDROOM TONIGHT. It's my second to last night here. The Annapurna range is right outside my bedroom, which has ceiling to floor windows on all four sides. My Kindle is dead. I can't charge anything. I am now reading weird books found in teahouses and dreaming ferocious dreams that are making me feel *oogey*. If I don't leave the light on in here, the bugs fly into my headlamp when I read. I am waking up every two or three hours in existential angst. Every night the guide tells me a little bit more about Nepalese culture and history. He also tells me about the mythology of the tribes here (including those that do and don't make it into the modern world). Hikers come and go of all types. I feel unmoored.

GURKA

At our final stop today a young Nepali girl brings a chicken into the dining room along with a yowling cat that settles on top of the counter where she can watch the whole group and still stay out of reach. The girl cradles the chicken in her lap and holds its beak now and again as if to keep it quiet while she sits with the adults and listens to them as they sit around the fire that is lit once a day in the early evening. These people eat what they grow so I am worried that she has brought the bird inside to kill it. I watched my mother do that once. She picked up a duck and with one fast motion broke its neck. An image of that happening to the chicken unnerves me. But the next morning I hear it clucking just outside the kitchen door. I look out my bedroom window to be sure it is the same bird. There are plenty of other chickens around her, but there she was stalking across the yard. So I don't have to cope with that bad memory today. I get more sensitive as we progress. I am hugely emotional react to everything as if I were seeing hardship for the first time in my life. It's dumb but that's what happens to me on these trips.

Today's trail was shitty. As we walk back down into the valleys we use the same paths that cattle and horses and buffalo use so you know, plop, plop. There are three kinds of leeches. One is a thin red kind that clings to leaves and stretches out horizontally and hooks onto creatures that brush by. Then there is a thin black kind that lives on the ground and crawls onto your shoes and works its way up into your socks. And then there is a big thick globular motherfucker that drops from overhead foliage onto the backs of your hands and arms.

My guide, who washes every day, is cleaner than me. I just keep trying to remember to brush my teeth once a day and I think my sweat smells funny.

Didn't want to turn the light off last night. I felt too alone to sit in the dark. And since the electricity ran all night long, I didn't.

The good news is that they had European toilets!!!! A private bathroom and tile!!! Yippee!!! It's amazing how few amenities can ease anxieties. Between one and three a.m. there was a frantic flurry of bug activity in my room, all the bugs were hyped up because of the light, then at four they all seemed to pick spot and settle down. I finished reading a 400 page-book so hideous that I won't even admit to the title.

I may leave all my clothes in Nepal (even my shoes) when I leave this time.

This morning after breakfast I spot a guy having his morning smoke just before he begins his trek today. We joke about that until his wife joins us and then we discuss how long you can go without taking a shower. I can't tell them exactly where I'm headed today because I can neither remember nor pronounce any of the names of the places we pass through. The couple said that it was easier for them to remember names because they are Indian and therefore have a more facile linguistic relationship with Nepali names. The wife tells me her name and then quickly says, "Just call me Cindy." The couple intended to climb Poon Hill this morning with the rest of us, but couldn't get themselves out of bed in time to see the sunrise. Lucky for them there wasn't one. Finally my guide signals me. We all wish each other well and head our separate ways.

After a couple of hours we take a break on the trail along with four twenty-somethings who are headed up top. One of the girls sits in the wet overgrown meadow near the cattle. NOPE. They promise my guide and me that we are near the end. I call them liars and promise them the same thing.

It's a good day.

Then we pass four Nepali women hiking up to forage in the forest. They'll spend the day at it and return by nightfall their baskets filled with vegetables and herbs. In a Nepalese exchange with my guide everyone realizes that the teahouse we will sleep in tonight is near the women's houses. In these villages everything is near everything else. My guide is invited for tea. Roosters are crowing on a regular basis all day long. As we near the next village I see colored prayer flags vertically aligned and posted on flagpoles. In a cornfield near the door of our teahouse six women churn the soil with short hoes, colorful skirts, sandals and headscarves. Loads of wet clothing and towels flutter everywhere on ubiquitous clotheslines. Three layer crustless sandwiches. My tuna sandwich tastes cinnamony. This business of me not wanting sugar in my tea (or milk or sugar in my coffee) makes the locals roll their eyes.

In Gurka the second story is used for storage. The first story is the living space. Slate roofs.

Young women, bright pink long-sleeved tops, dark yellow billowing pants. A beautiful woman squats over an orange tarp drying leaves which look like curled up bats when you see them in the forest. They are yellow when you pick them fresh, then they dry this grim grey-green color. She will sort them and somehow they will get mixed into the food chain in a way that has been explained to me more than once but I still don't understand.

My guide has shown me certain plants that the Nepalese use for medicines here. "This is for fever, very bitter. We make a paste and mix it with something or you will spit it out." He and I tend to arrive before or after the bulk of the trekking crowd. Either we are moving quickly or we don't stop where most people stop so they are gone (or we are) before the crowd arrives at the favorite spots. We have, on average, taken half the time the arranged schedule predicted. My guide says he has clients who take six slow steps and then ask how long it will take so that some treks "are very long." I try to explain why it is weird for me to say I am from America because in fact I am from Los Angeles. Then we discuss how people locate themselves when they define who they are. My guide says he gets quite a few Californian trekkers. Why now does my tea taste salty?

I stole this pen and I cannot lock my new bedroom door. I hope that it doesn't matter. Definitely gonna donate all my clothes when I get back to Pokhara. Feel a little queasy and constipated, but the big sickness is gone. I really didn't want to get on a plane as long as I was ill. 1000 rupees to tip the driver? 5000 for the guide? Also my calves are stunningly sore.

Slate roofs. Stacks of thin slate stone walls layered from the ground up. Dark narrow window frames, blue paint. Blue strips of color for the roofs if they aren't just grey. Piles of sticks, piles of wood stacked by the side of the house or stored in the second story sheds, small terraced gardens where they make their living with hand tools and a regimented rotation of crops along with some husbandry. Water is solar heated. Because of the small spaces and the importance of protecting what little they have, their animals although they are not pets share living spaces as often as not here. I don't know the rules exactly ... dogs outside, chickens and cats can be inside. Bigger animals stay in the fields right outside your window. Some must wander, it's the only way they can find enough to eat, but big animals all wear bells. Ducks and goats especially wander and I can see these are alternatively allowed supervised wandering and then are herded into total lockdown at night. Stone sidewalks, stone steps winding stairways everywhere. It only takes thirty minutes to walk the entire village, but it's a dazzling Dali picture puzzle when you stand up top on a hill and see the whole thing at once. It's a place that physically exists on several levels, a terraced town. The village dripping downhill to a flat spot before the valley takes another precipitous dive. All of it unfolds in a thick green gasp in between the forest sections.

Piles and piles of rocks all over town. Whenever money comes in for a construction project they build steps and schools and houses.

Step by step, little by little, the town is built up. In some places a rich man comes through and for whatever reason falls in love and spends his wealth bringing the town some modernity and a little stability.

Nepal gets its electricity, by in large, from India. It needs its water, but I see at least one hydroelectric power plant being built. Nepal depends on India for a number of necessary supplies but whenever India becomes angry with a Nepalese policy, it holds back provisions. The policy is encouraging Nepal to consider alternatives.

TREK INTO THE ANNAPURNA RANGE: MY LAST DAY

For your last night when a mentally fracturing type of exhaustion owns you, all the dogs in the valley will bark from 9 p.m. until 5 a.m. and this will bother no one else.

"Every night?" The villagers just smile and nod.

I am constitutionally incapable of sleeping if a dog needs something.

FIX IT. FIX IT. "What do they want? What do they need? Is it a tiger? Is it a bear? Is it Scott Bakula?" BARK. BARK. BARK. BARK. BARK. BARK. BARK. BARK. BARK. BARK.

Turn the iPod up! BARK. BARK. She's a woman in BARK. BARK. He's gonna break BARK pieces BARK ... don't want to see.

"Who's barking?"

Use earplugs. Muffled bark, bark, bark, bark.

"Why are they barking?"

Go outside to look at the dogs. BARK. BARK. BARK. BARK. "Why won't they stop? Make them stop."

Get up and get dressed (who the hell knows what the plan was there because I ain't trekking in the dark). Put on a headlamp and sit in the kitchen downstairs and stare into the dark like some sort of Stephen King villain. BARK. BARK. BARK. BARK.

FIX IT. FIX IT.

Undress. There's black mold in my bathroom and I think my underarms smell weird. Does Sean know how to set the sprinklers? BARK. BARK. BARK. BARK. I look wizened. At what point in time did my grandmother hijack my face?

Do something.

Pack. BARK. BARK. BARK. BARK. "Why do I own this?" Unpack (because I still need stuff).

FIX IT. FIX IT.

The room has a panoramic view of the mountains, but it is 10 sq. ft. with a cot. I am in a box. Box. Box. BARK. BARK. BARK. BARK. BARK. BARK. BARK. BARK.

I lose consciousness curled up in the bed holding my head and have a nightmare about holding my dog in my arms as he dies.

So, the next morning, it's oogey to be me.

For today 2 hours of stepping down. The slate steps, carved out of rock faces and installed by hand, are 6 to 24 inches high. Some are slick, but you can't tell this until you step on them (no medical insurance, I'd better be good at this). Some steps are mobile and roll away or just topple while you fight to stay upright. It rains intermittently (in sheets) for 20 minutes and then stops. The moisture invokes a rich bouquet of horse, buffalo, and goat shit that's been smoothed into a nice mash on the steps, but you're busy stepping down, stepping down, stepping down. I know the river and the car are at the end of this, but step, step, step.

We get to the car and it bumps along a series of connected ditches until we come to a squealing stop behind a stalled line of cars.

"Construction," the guide says as he and the driver get out.

"And?"

"We wait."

"Until they've finished building the road?"

He shrugs. "They work. And when they rest, we go." And then he and the driver fade into the crowd of newly minted pedestrians.

I lie down on something horizontal and cement like. A small toothless elf tries to sell me cucumber slices. A 12-year old Nepalese wearing a t-shirt that says "TUPACK Was" tries to sell me weird flavored chips. In fifteen minutes his follow-up will try to sell them to me for twice the price. They don't know that I've given up eating. I stop eating on treks and start having to bump up the nutritional value of my liquids. Trekking to Everest base camp narrowed me down to Fanta and hot black tea.

Finally.

The driver rushing us to our deaths, takes the narrow winding mountain road with an unprotected drop off at 65+ mph honking, but not slowing down, at every hair pin turn a soft fishtail slide. We're outpacing the FLYING paragliders on our left.

At the hotel I grab my bags before someone else tries to ransom them back to me. Shower. BARK. BARK. BARK.

HOME

FACT: You forget the place you leave behind. It's jarring to come back home. In fact it's harder to re-acclimate to the place you live than it is to adjust to a place you've never been before.

"Thinking is a kind of reason. Solving a puzzle but reason has to do with finding the grounds of being and the fundamental structure of the universe"

(Joseph Campbell, *The Power of Myth*)

Made in the USA
Las Vegas, NV
11 September 2022

55110235R00083